The Perfect fit

For Eva Howarth, born in Peking, trained in Paris and living in London and Cannes, dressmaking is a way of life. Her experience running the Paris salon of Maggie Rouff convinced her that most home dressmakers dream of having couture-class clothes on a mass-market budget, and over the years she has developed a system that anyone can use to make garments that fit exactly. The result is THE PERFECT FIT.

The Perfect fit

The unique formula for easy dressmaking

Eva Howarth

Hamlyn
London · New York · Sydney · Toronto

First published 1985
The Hamlyn Publishing Group Limited
London · New York · Sydney · Toronto
Astronaut House, Feltham, Middlesex, England
©Copyright Mary Vas

ISBN 0 600 345 61 X cased
ISBN 0 600 345 62 9 limp

A PHOEBE PHILLIPS EDITIONS BOOK
Set in England by Williamson Printing Ltd
Printed in Yugoslavia

Contents

Foreword

This book gives you all the information you need to produce a "couture" garment. The first part deals with the most basic problem faced by home dressmakers: how to achieve a perfect fit. Easy to follow instructions tell you how to make your own personal bodyprint to your own measurements, and how to use this bodyprint to alter commercial patterns so that you can make up a dress in the certain knowledge that the garment will fit you exactly. The second part consists of 24 lessons in dressmaking techniques that will enable you to finish your garment to couture standard.

Measurements are given in both imperial and metric. Remember that they are not interchangeable, and use either one or the other; continental patterns, from France or Germany for example, will have only metric measurements.

Finally, although most dressmaking terms are international, the following two points are worth noting. Vilene is a well-known brand name for a make of interfacing and Pellon is another equivalent brand name. Both come in a variety of weights. Tacking and basting are both temporary sewing stitches.

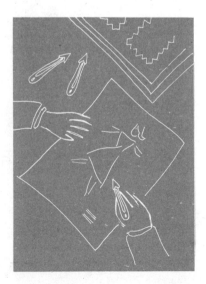

Introduction

Fashion today is international and it can be argued that Paris, traditionally the world capital of the art, has been overtaken, or at least equalled, by Rome, Milan, London and New York.

Nevertheless, the city's early supremacy is still reflected in fashion houses throughout the world. The very terms "couture" (applied to houses where the clothes are made to measure) and "haute couture" (used for houses which work exclusively from their own original designs) are obvious examples.

The creativity and standards of workmanship of the great Parisian couturiers—Worth, Chanel, Balenciaga, Dior and Yves St Laurent—have become equally international. A dress ordered from such a couture house anywhere in the world will be an original design, made to your measurements and perfectly finished. And when you receive your bill you will understand why very few women can afford to buy their clothes there.

It is no wonder that haute couture seems to many women a distant world, a dream seen in Vogue or Harpers Bazaar. Yet in one

important respect it is nearer to dressmaking at home than to other sections of the fashion industry. In both, clothes are made to measure. In between the two everything is mass produced.

For this very reason, the gulf between the couturier and the home dressmaker is not as wide as you might imagine, and this book provides a bridge across the gulf. Its aims are:

To enable anyone—even a beginner—to make clothes which look and fit as if they came from a couture house.

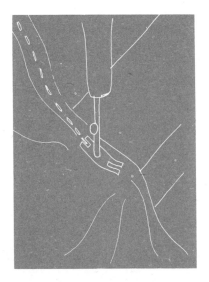

To make the process of learning as short and easy as possible.

To make dressmaking enjoyable.

To give you clothes, even on the slimmest budget, which fit you so well that you know you will always look your very best.

Couture and you

A couture house can produce beautiful, and beautifully finished, clothes because it has special skills. It is a team of experts headed by a designer. Between them they provide artistic talent for creating designs and technical expertise in cutting and making up.

The designer

In a couture house the most important figure is the designer.

For the home dressmaker design —even couture design—is something she can buy in the form of a good pattern.

They are available in shops throughout the world, and come from the best and most famous couture houses.

The fitter

Another important figure is the fitter, who gives a number of fittings to the client to make sure the garment looks perfect on her.

You will not be taught the skills of a fitter. To be really good at this needs years of training.

Instead in Part One you will learn to adjust patterns to your own measurements with such accuracy that the need for fittings and subsequent alterations is eliminated.

The dressmaker

The dressmaker has training in all the techniques involved in producing a perfect garment, and considerable experience in putting these into practice at couture level.

Many techniques are used in dressmaking. To become a really skilled professional dressmaker you would have to attend a course of instruction lasting two or three years and then serve an apprenticeship which might last even longer.

With the method I have used in this book, dressmaking is simplified and you will learn the techniques more quickly.

Experience and expertise

In a couture house, even the simplest job is done by an expert.

The home dressmaker is all too likely to go out and buy her pattern and material (perhaps very expensive material) and then start to make her dress, learning the necessary techniques as she goes along. The result, all too often, is a dress that just doesn't look anything like the picture on the pattern envelope, doesn't fit

properly and is used as a house dress or is worn outside only when it can be covered by a coat.

However there is an alternative. Dressmaking, like other crafts, is based on a limited number of basic principles.

In Part Two you will be taught these basic principles, the essentials of dressmaking, and shown how to apply them to a variety of different problems. For example, in one lesson you will be told how to make up and attach collars.

You will be shown first how to make up the simplest form of collar and how to attach it to the neckline of a garment.

You will then learn how the same principles can be applied to more sophisticated styles.

As you go along, you will see that all collars are only variations on the same basic principle, which you will find easy to learn and easy to put into practice.

No one would dream of trying to make a lobster soufflé if they only knew how to scramble eggs. So, before you start making up a garment, consider all the techniques you will need. Have you acquired the necessary expertise for each of these?

Perhaps you feel sure that you have. But if not, Part Three shows you how to practise first on calico cut-outs made from minipatterns until you are satisfied with the results.

In this way you will learn the necessary expertise and each dress will bring you added confidence in your skills.

The ability to choose a pattern and fabric

In a couture house the designer chooses the materials for all the dresses in his collection.

Just as you can buy a pattern, so you can buy materials, but learning to choose the right pattern and the material to go with it is as important as acquiring dressmaking skills.

When choosing a pattern, your first consideration will be its style. This is a question of taste. But there are other considerations, no less important, to bear in mind.

It has already been emphasised that you must become an expert in particular skills before you start making a garment. You should therefore look at any pattern which you want to buy in this light.

Are any techniques involved which you have not mastered?

Will you need more practice in these? If so, are you prepared to spend time in learning them before you start work?

If you are in any doubt, choose an easier pattern rather than risk failure—each success will help you to the next one.

Choosing a material is one of the most difficult tasks for dress-makers at all levels.

When you look at an illustration in a pattern book or fashion magazine, you see a combination of style and material. Any style will always look best in the type of material in which it was originally made up.

It is not always easy to tell what the material is just by looking at the illustration.

You will learn to ask yourself many questions, such as:

Is the fabric light-, medium- or heavyweight?

Is it transparent?

Does it look as though it will stretch?

Does it hang softly in drapes?

The answers should enable you to buy material similar to the one you like in the pattern book or magazine.

Extras

In a couture house great care is exercised in choosing the extras for a dress. These may be belts, buttons, lining, interfacing, sewing thread—everything in fact that is needed to make a garment. Later in this book, under appropriate headings, you will learn how these extras should be chosen.

Home couture

Is it possible to make "couture" clothes for yourself?

The answer can be "yes"— provided you approach the problem in the right way.

In Part One of this book you will learn how to adjust any pattern to your own measurements. In Part Two you will learn the essentials of good dressmaking in 24 lessons.

Finally, always remember that the simple, perhaps even rather obvious, points we have made are essential guidelines if you are to bridge the gulf between couture and home dressmaking.

A NEW SYSTEM

Summary of Part One

The biggest single problem which a woman who makes her own clothes will normally have to face is how to fit herself.

Part One of this book will not show you how to fit yourself. Instead, it will tell you how you can eliminate the problem entirely.

This is made possible by a new system never explained in book form before.

The system is summarized in this chapter to show you how simple and effective it is.

A new pattern

When a new pattern is created it begins with a sketch by the designer. This is handed over to the head fitter. It is the head fitter's responsibility to produce a perfect pattern, from which she will be able to cut and make up the model exactly as the designer conceived it.

The essential principles which govern the making of a pattern can be explained very simply.

The fitter takes a basic pattern

The basic pattern (below left) is made up of standard body measurements plus what is known as basic ease. This basic ease allows for movement.

The fitter will have a basic pattern in every size in her stock.

As you see, the basic pattern has no particular style. It simply follows the body outline.

She adds designer's ease

To make up a dress which has a distinct style additional material is needed. This is known as designer's ease. Clearly the amount of the designer's ease will vary according to the style.

Once she has calculated the extra amount of material needed for the particular style she is working on, the fitter will add it to the basic pattern (below centre).

Basic ease provides the comfort of a dress, designer's ease its style.

The finished pattern

The finished pattern (below right) shows only the final outlines and some important guidelines.

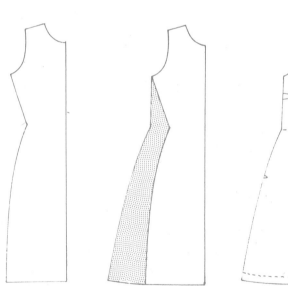

 *DESIGNER'S EASE*

DIFFERENCE BETWEEN STANDARD MEASUREMENTS AND YOUR OWN MEASUREMENTS

At one time a couture house's patterns were used exclusively for its clients. Today a number of them are bought by pattern companies and made available to shops throughout the world.

If you are a perfect standard size

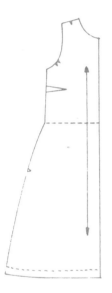

You may be one of the rare people blessed with a perfect standard size. If so your measurements will coincide exactly with those of the basic pattern.

When you make up a dress there is no need for you to adjust the pattern.

The dress will feel comfortable and look as the designer intended it.

If you are not a standard size

If you are not a standard size, your measurements will differ in one or more places from the basic pattern.

The illustration below left shows the difference between your own measurements and the basic pattern.

The illustration below centre shows what happens when you make up a dress pattern which is not right for you.

In order to accommodate your own measurements you are using some of the designer's ease.

Infringing on the designer's ease means that there will not be enough material to produce the particular style chosen.

The dress will not look as the designer intended it. It will not feel right either. In other words, failure.

What can you do?

The obvious solution—and the correct one—is to adjust the pattern to your own measurements. In this example it means enlarging the pattern.

The amount you have to add to your dress pattern is the difference between your own measurements and the basic pattern.

This is really very easy, for you can apply the alteration directly to the edge of your pattern. (See the illustration below right.)

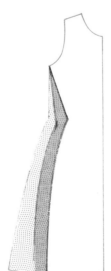
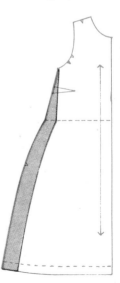

A new system

It has already been explained that to adjust a pattern to your own measurements with complete accuracy you have to:

Find the exact difference between your own and standard measurements.

Apply these differences on to the edge of your dress pattern.

You will learn to do this in a few easy stages.

Buy a basic pattern

You can buy these at the pattern counter of department stores.

Make the basic pattern up in calico

Any pattern made up in calico is called a toile.

Adjust the toile to your own measurements

Later in the book you will be shown how to do this step by step.

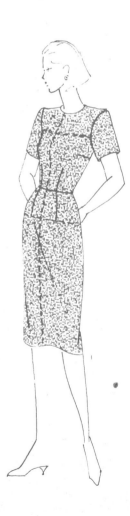

Compare the adjusted toile with the basic pattern

To do this, you must first take your toile to pieces. Then place each piece on a corresponding piece of the basic pattern.

You can now see the differences between your own measurements and the standard size.

You will need this information every time you buy a new pattern. For this reason you will want to have a permanent record of it.

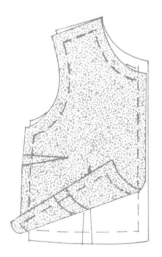

CALICO	
BODYPRINT	
YOUR BODY SHAPES	
STANDARD MEASUREMENTS	
YOUR OWN MEASUREMENTS	

Draw a picture of your findings

Take a sheet of paper and place all the pieces of your basic pattern on it.

Draw round each pattern-piece with a ballpoint pen. Then remove the pattern-pieces.

Place the corresponding pieces of the toile on top of each pattern-piece you have just drawn. With a contrasting coloured ballpoint pen draw round each piece of toile.

Remove the pieces of the toile.

The picture which you have now drawn is known as a bodyprint. It shows the difference between your own measurements and the basic pattern.

The differences—the shaded areas on the bodyprint—are called body shapes or simply shapes.

To adjust any dress pattern to your own measurement you simply copy the shapes on to the corresponding places on the edge of your pattern.

You do this with the help of a simple formula, which you will find on the next page.

BODYPRINT

BODYPRINT

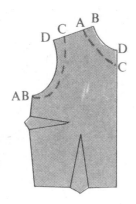

As you can see, shapes differ greatly in appearance. But they all have either four sides or three.

You need concern yourself only with the two shortest sides of the shapes, A-B and C-D or, in the case of three-sided shapes, point AB and C-D.

The formula

To copy your shapes on to any pattern, irrespective of style:

Measure A-B on your bodyprint.

Measure the same distance on the corresponding place on your pattern and mark point A.

Measure C-D on your bodyprint.

Measure the same distance on the corresponding place on your pattern and mark point C.

Join A to C on the pattern, following the pattern outline.

PATTERN TO BE ADJUSTED (BODICE WITH SQUARE NECK)

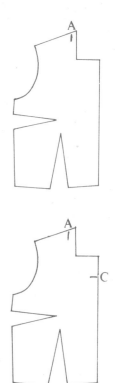

BODYPRINT

The formula

PATTERN TO BE ADJUSTED
(BODICE WITH V-NECK)

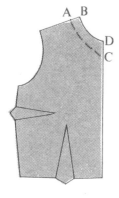

Measure A-B on your bodyprint.

Measure the same distance on
the corresponding place on your
pattern and mark point A.

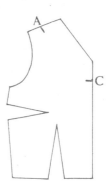

Measure C-D on your bodyprint.

Measure the same distance on
your pattern and mark point C.

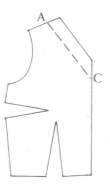

Join A to C on the pattern,
following the pattern outline.

15

To adjust a whole pattern to your
own measurements you copy
each shape in turn from the
bodyprint on to your dress pattern.
You always use the same formula
in exactly the same way.

BODYPRINT

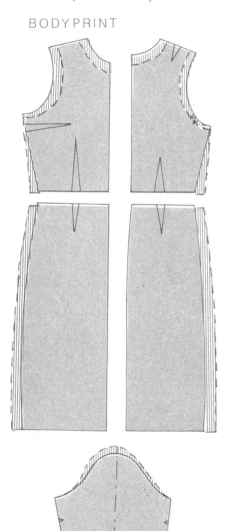

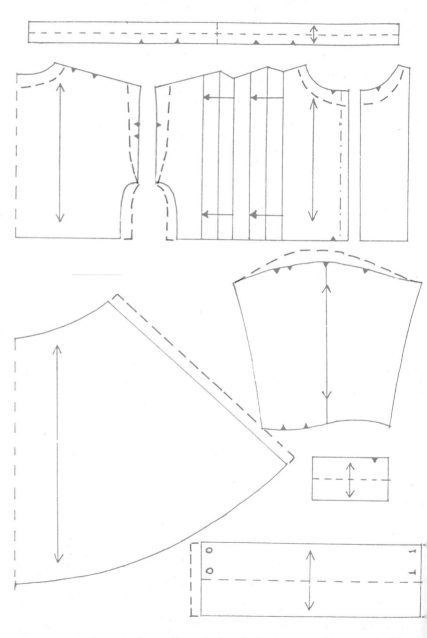

16

FINISHED GARMENT

Advantages of this method

You have to fit yourself only once in a lifetime. This is when you make your toile.

With the help of this book you will find adjusting a toile to your own measurements much easier than you expected.

Your bodyprint can last you for ever.

If your figure alters over the years, you can easily adjust your bodyprint accordingly.

You make all alterations on the edge of your pattern. This is much easier than the conventional way of cutting into patterns.

The system works so accurately that once a pattern has been adjusted no further alterations are needed during the making up of the garment.

In other words, the agony so often experienced by the home dressmaker when trying to fit herself and make endless alterations is eliminated.

You will be using exactly the same formula in exactly the same way for every pattern and can be certain that if it has worked once it will work every time.

A great deal of time and aggravation are saved, and dressmaking becomes fun.

Knowing that the end result will be perfect, you can safely buy good materials with no danger of wasting them.

The system works equally for the experienced dressmaker and the complete beginner.

It can be applied to coats, jackets, dresses, blouses, skirts.

It works equally well for all makes of pattern (American, Continental or British).

The essence of the system can be summed up in a single sentence: You never have to fit a dress on yourself and you always get perfect results.

Note:
See pages 44-45 for a complete step-by-step summary of how to adjust your dress pattern.

PART ONE

MAKING AND USING A BODYPRINT

This section of the book explains in detail the five easy stages described in the summary on the previous pages.

Buy a basic pattern

Your first task is to go out and buy a basic pattern in your size.

To carry out the instructions in Part One you will also need:

3½ yards (3 metres) of 36-inch (90-cm) width medium-weight unbleached calico.

2¼ yards (2 metres) medium-weight "sew-on" Vilene.

Three different-coloured ballpoint pens.

Your correct size

The pattern size you need is determined by your bust measurement!

Take your measurement at the fullest part of your bust.

Hold the tape-measure level at both front and back.

To ensure that you are measuring correctly allow enough ease for the tape-measure to be moved forward and backward across your bust.

If you are between sizes, choose the larger size pattern.

It is advisable to buy a basic pattern which includes more than one bodice front and which caters for bust sizes A, B, C and D.

Choose the pattern size which corresponds with your bra.

Different makes of basic pattern

Most major pattern companies produce a basic pattern of their own, which you can buy at the pattern counter of stores.

The sizings used by different companies sometimes vary. This need not worry you.

For your immediate needs, buy a basic pattern in the make you are likely to use most frequently.

At a later stage you will be shown how to make allowance for the different makes of pattern, which sometimes vary in sizing and proportion.

The basic pattern you bought

The pattern which you will be using for making up your toile will have been sold to you in a normal pattern envelope.

Inside the envelope you will find:
    Your pattern
    A lay-out plan
    Instructions on how to make up your toile

Some pattern envelopes include variations on the basic pattern and have pattern-pieces (marked B, C or D) relating to these variations.

When making up your toile you should ignore all these and concern yourself only with the pattern-pieces which relate to the basic pattern. These are normally marked A.

You will use the five main pattern-pieces only:
  Bodice front
  Bodice back
  Skirt front
  Skirt back
  Sleeve

Markings on your pattern:

The cutting line   _____
The sewing line   — — — — —
Balance marks, which are usually numbered

Every balance mark has a counterpart on one of the other pattern-pieces. When pattern-pieces are joined balance marks must meet.

Fold line

Opening for a zip

The front and back of a sleeve or an armhole.

Cut out your pattern-pieces

Each pattern-piece has a cutting line and a sewing line clearly shown on it, as well as various other markings.

Transfer all markings from the cutting line to the sewing line. Cut out the pattern-pieces along the sewing lines.

This may seem strange to you, but there is a good reason for it.

The normal practice is to cut out the pattern-pieces along the cutting line (top right).
By this method, when you place a pattern-piece on your fabric and draw round it, all you can mark on the fabric is the cutting line.

With our system you cut out your pattern-pieces along the sewing line (bottom right). Therefore, when you place a pattern-piece on your fabric and draw round it, you are marking the sewing line on your fabric.

You then measure on the fabric a distance of 1 inch (2.5 cm) all around on the outside of the sewing line and mark your cutting line there.

Having your sewing line marked on your fabric will make your dressmaking much easier, quicker and more accurate.

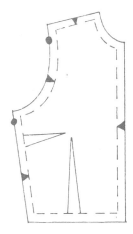

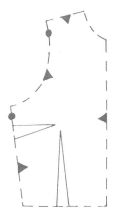

Size chart in inches and centimetres

Bust size		inches	31½	32½	34	36	38	40	42
		cm	80	83	87	92	97	102	107
Pattern size (American)			6	8	10	12	14	16	18
Pattern size (British)			8	10	12	14	16	18	20
Pattern size (Continental)			36	38	40	42	44	46	48

Make the basic pattern up in calico

Any pattern made up in calico is called a toile

The instructions given in this chapter apply only to the making of a toile. A toile is not intended to be worn as a dress, and for this reason certain liberties can be taken which would not be tolerated in real dressmaking.

Lay out your calico

Use the largest table you have and a cutting-board if possible. (See equipment, page 126.)

Material is normally laid out with the reverse side up. With calico it hardly matters as the difference between the reverse and the right side is so slight.

Unless the layout guide tells you otherwise, lay out your material (calico) lengthways and fold it in two so that the two long edges meet and lie parallel with the straight lines on your cutting-board.

To hold the two layers together put a few pins both in the main body of the calico and along the edges.

Lay out your pattern

Lay the pattern-pieces on top of your calico with the printed side up.

Remember that you have trimmed your pattern-pieces to the sewing line. You must therefore leave space (about 4 inches / 10cm) between the pattern-pieces for seam allowances.

Most basic patterns have a seam in the centre back of both the bodice and the skirt.

When making up a toile you must have the centre front, as well as the centre back, of the bodice and skirt clearly marked. The best way of doing this is to create seams in the front too.

Remember to leave space for seam allowances at the newly created seams.

Pattern-pieces should be placed so that the centre front and centre back of both bodice and skirt lie parallel with the long edge of the calico. The same applies to the centre line of the sleeves.

> **If your hips are much larger than your bust, leave an extra inch or two between the pattern-pieces.**

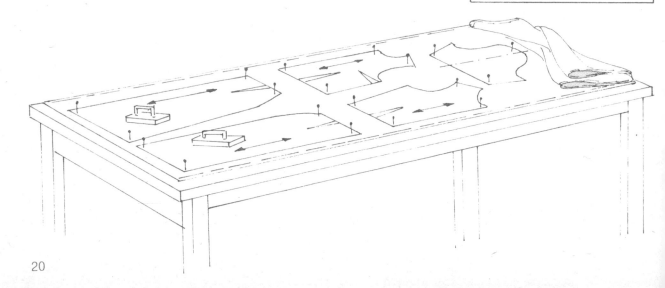

Keep the pattern-pieces in position with pins and weights. For weights you can use ashtrays or any other suitable objects that happen to be handy.

Mark your sewing line on the calico

Use coloured ballpoint pens. Draw around each pattern-piece.

Use one colour for marking all sewing lines as well as darts and balance marks.

Do not use the same colour for any other purpose when marking or making your toile.

Mark your cutting line on the calico

Mark your cutting line at the edge of your seam allowances, using a different coloured ballpoint pen.

Seam allowances on dresses are usually 1 inch (2.5 cm). For making up a toile the seam allowances are different:

Leave 1 inch (2.5 cm) seam allowance at the armholes and sleeve tops.

Leave 2 inches (5 cm) seam allowance on all other seams. Leave no seam allowance at neckline.

Once you have finished marking remove the pins and weights which have been holding the

pattern in place, and lift the pattern off.

Pin the two layers of calico together, placing pins along the sewing lines and all markings. At corners pin as shown on the diagram below.

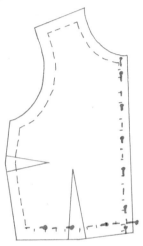

Cut out the calico

Remember to cut along the cutting lines and not the sewing lines.

Mark the bottom layer of the calico

You have cut out two layers of fabric for each pattern-piece, but have marked only the top layer.

The bottom layer must also be marked. To do this:

Turn over the two layers of calico which you have pinned together.

Use a ballpoint pen to mark between the pins as in the diagram below. Use the same colour as you did for marking the top layer of the calico.

Make sure you mark the corners accurately.

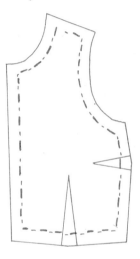

Remove all the pins and separate the two layers of calico.

You have now finished marking and cutting out the calico for your toile.

Your next step is to make up your toile.

In Part Two of this book you will learn the essentials of good dressmaking. At this stage the information you are given is being kept to a minimum. It amounts simply to what you need to know in order to make up your own toile successfully.

Basic sewing

Whenever you join two pieces of material together, you should follow the five main steps in sewing. These are: pin, tack, stitch, press, trim.

Pin

When pinning together two pieces of material, make sure that the sewing line of one is exactly on top of the sewing line of the other.

Pin through both layers of material with the pins lying lengthways along the sewing line.

Tack

Tacking is a temporary joining of two pieces of material. For this you use a running stitch. (See page 78.) When you have finished tacking remove the pins.

Stitch

You can, if you wish, sew a dress entirely by hand, but it is obviously quicker to do it by machine.

Sewing by machine is referred to here as "stitching".

The bulk of the material which you are working on should lie to the left-hand side of the foot of the sewing machine. Hold and guide your material with both hands when stitching. One hand should be behind the needle and one in front.

When you have finished stitching remove the tacking threads.

Always stitch on the reverse side of the material.

Adjust your sewing machine to a fairly long stitch. This will make unpicking easier when alterations are needed.

Press

Every time you stitch a seam you should immediately press the seam open. Always press on the reverse side of the fabric.

Do not use a damp cloth or a steam iron for pressing calico. If you do the calico will shrink.

Trim

Do not trim until you are sure that all the alterations needed have been completed. Otherwise you may find you have not left yourself enough material to do the work.

Make up your toile

The order in which you should make up your toile is: the bodice, the sleeves, and finally the skirt.

The bodice

First make up the darts, both in the front and the back of the bodice.

Pin the dart together at the sewing line, starting in the seam allowance 1/4 inch (6 mm) from the sewing line. Always start at the widest part and work towards the narrowest, to the point of the dart.

Tack, stitch.

Leave all waist darts open below the waistline.

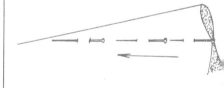

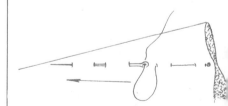

Press. Always press vertical darts towards the centre front or centre back, and horizontal darts downwards.

Once you have completed the darts join up the bodice in the following order: front, shoulders and side seams.

Leave the side seams open below the waistline.

For each seam follow the standard instructions: pin, tack, stitch, press.

The sleeve

Stitch (by machine) two lines in the seam allowance of the sleeve.

Join the under-arm seams.

With the right sides of the calico together, place the sleeve in the armhole so that the front of the sleeve meets the front of the bodice and the back of the sleeve meets the back of the bodice.

From here on work from the inside of the sleeve.

Make sure that all balance marks meet.

Place pins at right angles to the sewing lines.

On one side of the sleeves pull up both gathering threads between balance marks A and B so that the circumference of the sleeve and that of the armhole become the same.

Secure the gathering threads by winding both ends around a pin in a figure of 8.

With the tip of a pin distribute fullness evenly between balance marks and secure with more pins.

Repeat the procedure on the other side of the sleeve.

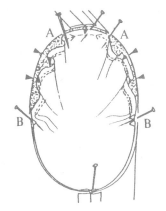

Tack the sleeve into the armhole.

Stitch with the sleeve lying uppermost.

Turn the seam allowances towards the armholes.

To insert the zip

Use a zip 20 inches (54 cm) long. Turn over the seam allowances at the centre back. Tack and press.

Pin the closed zip into position. The two edges of the calico should meet along the centre of the zip.

Open the zip and tack it into place. With the zip still open sew it in firmly by hand.

Skirt

Stitch up all the darts. Join up the seams in the following order: centre front, centre back (leaving an opening for the zip as marked), side seams. Press.

Leave all vertical seams and darts open from the waist up.

Do not join the skirt to the bodice at this stage.

Adjust the toile to your own measurements

Once you have completed sewing up the sections of your toile you are ready to make the necessary alterations.

This is the part of dressmaking you will probably approach with most anxiety.

There is really no need to worry. In this chapter you will find illustrations of every problem you are likely to meet and an explanation of how to put it right.

First some general rules

Never try on your toile when it is only held together with pins. The fitting will not be accurate.

Deal with only one alteration at a time.

Don't worry because you think this may slow you down. In reality you will end up working faster and more accurately.

When you have completed a particular alteration, try on the toile and make sure you are satisfied with the result. Only then should you move on to the next alteration.

Mark alterations on only one half of the toile while you have it on.

Start with the bodice, and only when it has been successfully altered, join the skirt on to the bodice and then fit the skirt.

Always work from the top down—neckline, then shoulder, and so on—and continue downwards finishing at the hem.

Never make any alterations at the centre front or centre back seams of your toile, either on the bodice or on the skirt.

If the measurements on one side of your body are different from those on the other side, see page 26 before you continue.

Altering your toile

Look at yourself in a mirror to see where the toile does not fit you properly.

On pages 27 to 37 you will find a section on faults and remedies. The illustrations show the different ways in which a toile may not fit. Next to the picture of the fault you will see a picture of the alteration you will need—the remedy.

1. The bodice on the right is too tight around the midriff and the remedy is to let it out at the side seams.

2. Mark the alteration on your toile.

Use pins to mark the alteration.

Make sure the pins are firmly secured and do not fall out. Mark only one side of the toile—the left or right hand—while you have it on. Indicate clearly the starting and finishing point of each alteration.

3. Transfer the markings to the reverse side of your toile.

Take off the toile. Turn it to the reverse side and mark between the pins with a ballpoint pen. Remember to mark clearly the starting and finishing points.

4. Copy the markings on to the other half of your toile.

Make sure that the markings are identical on both halves of the toile.

5. Carry out the alterations.

Carry out the alterations indicated on both halves of the toile.

When you have done this, stitch the toile up and try it on again. If you are satisfied with the result, go on to the next alteration.

TOILE	
REVERSE SIDE OF TOILE	
PINS	•–•–•
ORIGINAL SEWING LINE	–––––
ALTERATION LINE	––––

Side effects

Few people realize that when they make an alteration they may be bringing about a chain reaction of new problems. For example, lifting a shoulder seam may also cause the neckline to become raised, the bust dart to come too high, the waist to pull up. So making that first alteration has created three new problems.

It is these "side effects" which can cause much of the frustration home dressmakers experience.

This is also the reason why you should deal with only one alteration at a time.

The illustrations on pages 28 to 37 show faults and remedies with their possible side effects and how these should be put right.

After you have taken off your toile and transferred your markings to the reverse side of the fabric, mark the remedies for the side effects there too.

Deal with only one alteration and its side effects before you move on to the next.

For every fault in your toile that requires an alteration, follow this procedure.

Different measurements

You may be one of the many people whose measurements are not the same on both sides of your body.

In that case, first follow the instructions, disregarding for the moment the differences in measurements. Adjust your toile to the left side of your body, and alter the right side in the same way, even if it doesn't seem to fit.

When you have finished altering your bodice the left side should fit perfectly, but the right will need additional changes.

Now refit the right side, taking care to leave the left side exactly as it was. You will find further information on page 38.

Why a toile is essential

You may be wondering why you are expected to go to the trouble of making up and fitting a toile in order to discover the difference between your own and the standard measurements.

Could you not get the same results by using a tape-measure and comparing your own measurements with those of the basic pattern?

You can take your measurements easily enough when you are standing still. But your dress must look good and feel comfortable when you are moving about, raising your arms, bending or sitting down.

The measurements you need for doing all this can only come from a well-fitted toile and not by using a tape-measure.

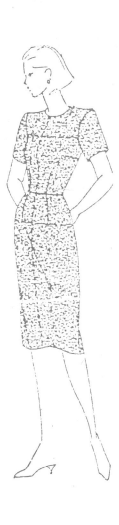

Faults and remedies

In the following pages you will see examples of the commonest faults in the way a toile fits (a).

Do not be alarmed by the nuymber of faults illustrated. Only a few are likely to concern you.

Next to the fault is shown the remedy (b).

Next to the remedy you can see the side effects which correcting the fault may produce and how to put them right to achieve the perfect fit (c).

The illustrations explain what you have to do. Only you can judge the amount of the alteration needed, for instance how much material you must add or take away. You have, however, one infallible guide to this.

On your toile you will have marked, or should have marked, both the vertical and horizontal grain lines, as shown in the illustration. A fault in the toile will have the effect of distorting a grain line.

A correction has been satisfactorily made only when the toile feels thoroughly comfortable and the grain lines are in the right position, either exactly vertical or exactly horizontal.

1

a) THE NECKLINE IS TOO HIGH AT THE FRONT

b) Lower the neckline.

c) Adjust the neckline at the point of the shoulder seam.

a   b   c

2

a) THE NECKLINE IS TOO LOOSE AT THE FRONT

b) Open up the shoulder seam. Move the front of the bodice along the shoulder until the neckline lies flat.

c) Adjust at the neckline and the armhole.

a   b   c

3

a) THE NECKLINE IS TOO LOW

b) With the help of your paper pattern cut out a new neckline of the right size. Tack the new neckline into position.

c) Adjust the neckline.

  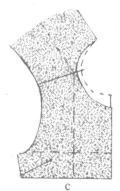

a   b   c

4

a) THE DRESS IS TOO TIGHT
AT THE BUST POINT

b) Open up the bust dart and
shorten it. The point of the dart
should lie about ½ inch (1 cm)
from the bust point.

c) Move the waist dart sideways
the same distance as that by
which you shortened the bust dart.

 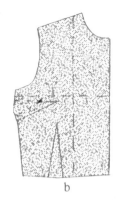 

a   b   c

5

a) THERE IS EXCESS FULLNESS
AT THE BUST POINT

b) Reduce the bust dart.

c) Shorten the side seam by the
same amount as the alteration in
the bust dart and correct the
armhole.

 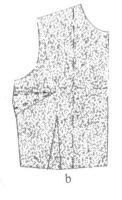 

a   b   c

6

a) THERE IS EXCESS FULLNESS
BELOW THE BUST DART

b) Enlarge the lower part of the
dart until the excess fullness
disappears.

c) Extend the top of the side seam
by the width with which you
enlarged the dart.

 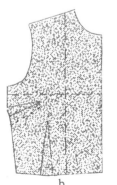 

a   b   c

7

a) THE BODICE IS TOO LOOSE

b) Take in at the side seam.

c) Make the same alteration at the back of the bodice, if necessary. You may also have to alter the armhole at the front and back.

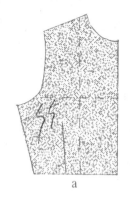  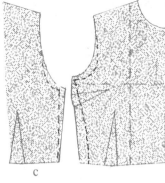

a   b   c

8

a) THE SHOULDER SEAM IS TOO SHORT

b) Lengthen the shoulder seam and correct the armhole.

c) Make the same alteration on the back of the bodice.

 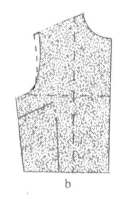 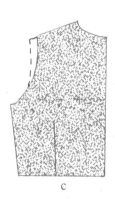

a   b   c

9

a) THE ARMHOLE IS TOO LOW

b) Extend the side seam and correct the armhole.

c) Make the same alteration on the back of the bodice.

a   b   c

10

a) THERE IS EXCESS FULLNESS
AT THE ARMHOLE

b) Lift the shoulder seam and take
in at the side seam.

c) Correct the armhole.

11

a) THE BODICE IS TOO TIGHT
BETWEEN THE ARMHOLE AND
THE BUST DART
(The armhole is distorted)

b) Enlarge the top of the dart until
all the tightness disappears and
the armhole lies smoothly around
the arm.

c) Extend the top of the side seam
by the same length as that of the
alteration at the dart. Correct the
armhole.

12

a) THE TOP OF THE BODICE IS
TOO WIDE

b) Take out the excess fabric at
the armhole.

c) Make the same alteration on the
back of the bodice.

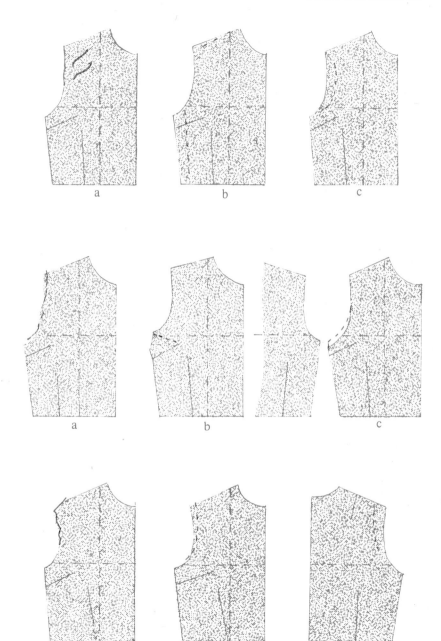

13

a) THE BODICE PULLS FROM THE SHOULDER

b) Extend the armhole as required. Redraw the shoulder seam.

c) Make the same alteration on the back of the bodice.

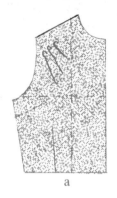  

a   b   c

14

a) THE BODICE HANGS LOOSE FROM THE SHOULDER

b) Take up the excess fullness into the shoulder seam.

c) Make the same alteration on the back of the bodice.

a   b   c

15

a) THE BODICE IS TOO LONG

b) Shorten the bodice.

c) Make the same alteration on the back of the bodice.

 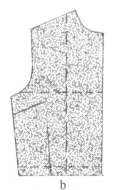 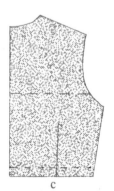

a   b   c

16

a) THE BODICE IS TOO TIGHT
AROUND THE MIDRIFF

b) Let out the side seam.

c) Make the same alteration on the
back of the bodice, if necessary.

17

a) THE TOP OF THE BODICE IS
TOO LONG

b) Take off the required amount
along the shoulder seam.

c) Lower the front of the neckline
by the same length as that of the
alteration at the shoulder seam.
Make the same alteration at the
back of the bodice, if necessary.

18

a) THE BODICE IS TIGHT
ACROSS THE SHOULDER
BLADE

b) Enlarge the dart and make sure
that it is now pointing exactly at the
shoulder blade.

c) Extend the shoulder seam by
the same length as the alteration
to the dart.

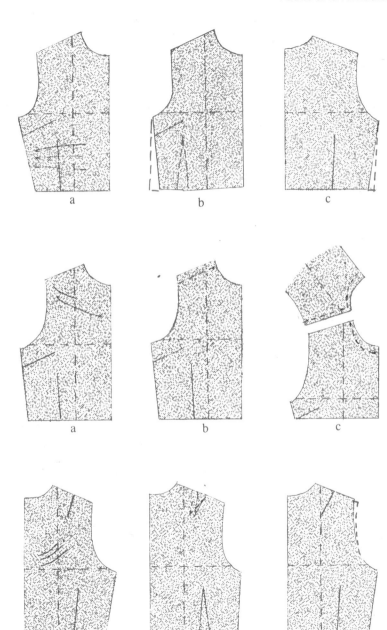

19

a) THE BODICE IS TOO WIDE
ACROSS THE ARMHOLE

b) Enlarge the armhole.

c) Make the same alteration at the
back of the armhole.

a   b   c

20

a) THE SLEEVE IS DRAGGING
AND FEELS TIGHT ACROSS
THE FRONT OF THE ARM

b) Open the sleeve and let it drop
until all dragging ceases.

Enlarge the top of the sleeve so
that it meets the armhole.

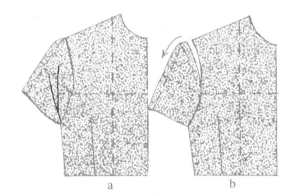

a   b

21

a) THE SLEEVE IS DROPPING
ALONG THE CENTRE LINE

b) Pin out the excess fabric.

Shorten the sleeve by the amount
you have pinned out.

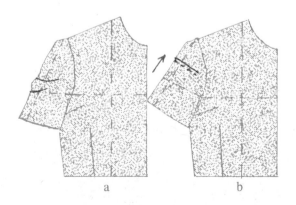

a   b

22

a) THE SLEEVE IS TIGHT
ACROSS THE ARM

b) Cut the sleeve open along the
centre line. Measure the amount
of extra material needed.

Cut a piece of calico accordingly
and fit it in the space.

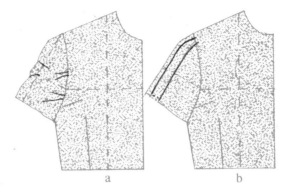
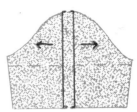

a   b

23

a) THE SLEEVE IS TOO WIDE

b) Pin out the excess fullness.

Cut open the sleeve along the
centre line, and take away the
amount of fabric you pinned out.

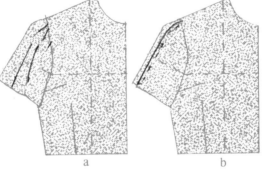
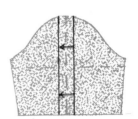

a   b

24

a) THE SLEEVE IS TIGHT
ACROSS THE ELBOW (1)

b, c) Lower the darts so that they
are opposite the elbow. You may
have to fit in an extra piece of
calico.

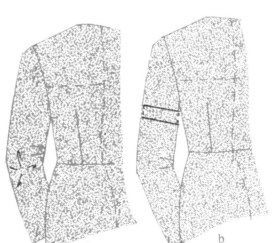
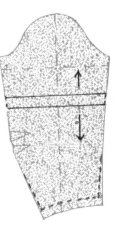

a   b

25

a) THE SLEEVE IS TIGHT ACROSS THE ELBOW (2)

b) Pin out excess length in the upper arm so that the darts are opposite the elbow.

Cut open the sleeve and take away the amount of fabric you pinned out.

26

a) THE SKIRT IS RIDING UP AT THE BACK

b) Extend the top of the skirt at the centre back so that it hangs correctly.

Redraw the waistline at the back of the skirt.

27

a) THE SKIRT IS RIDING UP AT THE FRONT

b) Extend the top of the skirt at the side seam so that it hangs correctly.

Redraw the waist seam.

28

a) THE SKIRT IS TIGHT ACROSS
THE BOTTOM

b) Open up along the centre and
side seam and let the skirt out the
required amount.

29

a) THE SKIRT IS TIGHT ACROSS
THE HIPS

b) Open up along the side seam
and let the skirt out the required
amount at the front and back.

30

a) THE SKIRT IS TOO BIG
AROUND THE HIPS

b) Take in the required amount
along the side seams at the front
and back.

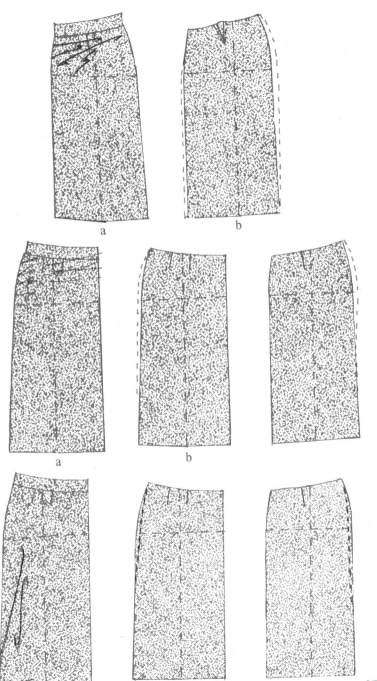

Compare the adjusted toile with the basic pattern

Your toile has now been adjusted to your own measurements

You will appreciate how important it is that your toile fits you perfectly.

If there is still a fault it will appear again and again in every dress you make for yourself.

So have one final look at your toile with very critical eyes. Move normally, bend a little, and walk around.

Does it look good?

Is it really comfortable?

If you are satisfied on all counts you can start on your next task.

Compare your toile with the basic pattern you bought

To do so, you first have to take the toile to pieces.

Remove the zip.

Open up the centre front and centre back seams.

If your measurements are the same on both sides of your body, put aside one half (left or right) of the toile. You will not need this.

If the measurements on one side of your body differ from those on the other, keep both halves of your toile.

The instructions which follow should be carried out on both halves. Before you do this mark every part of your toile "right" or "left".

Separate the bodice from the skirt. Remove the sleeves. Open all seams, including darts.

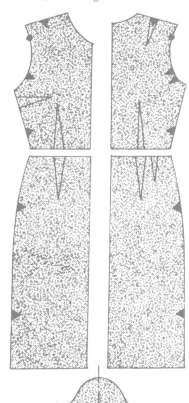

Press, taking great care not to stretch or shrink the calico. Do not use steam or a damp cloth.

Cut off all seam allowances. But first make sure that you don't cut off any balance marks.

If you want to see how you differ from the standard size, compare the original basic pattern with the corresponding pieces of your toile.

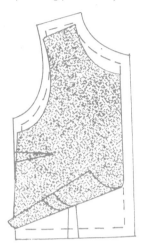

You will need this information every time you buy a new pattern. So you will want a permanent record of it.

How you get this is explained overleaf.

How to cope with making and adjusting your toile by yourself

You may well be wondering whether you can make a toile and adjust a pattern, as described in this book, all by yourself or whether you need the help of a friend.

The answer is that you can do it by yourself, though there is one stage in the process where the presence of a friend, though not necessary, could be helpful.

What you do need is a mirror in which you can see both your front and your back view at the same time. Two mirrors placed at an angle can achieve the same effect.

Finding your correct pattern size. For this you have to take your bust measurement, which you can easily do by yourself.

Making up your toile. This too you can manage by yourself.

Deciding on faults in the toile and finding the remedy. This is no more difficult than following instructions in a picture book. You ought not to need any help.

Fitting yourself. This is where you may find yourself in difficulties. As any woman who has ever tried knows, to mark certain alterations

on a toile or a dress while you are actually wearing it is virtually impossible. There are places, such as the middle of the back, which you simply cannot reach. Also, every time you move you alter your body outline.

What you must therefore do is, first, to mark the alterations at points which you can reach easily, that is at the front of the bodice. Then for the other alterations, you estimate the amount needed. After that you take off your toile, mark the alterations with pins, put the toile on again, and see whether the proposed alteration is right. Here a friend could help you, but such help is not absolutely necessary. You can manage by yourself, though some patience may be needed.

Marking alterations to the reverse side of the material and carrying them out. Here you ought to have no difficulty.

Drawing your bodyprint. Again no difficulty as you will see on the following pages. Once you have your bodyprint you will be able to adjust any pattern to your own measurements without the need for any further fittings. In other words, your difficulties are over.

Your bodyprint

A drawing which shows all the differences between your own measurements and the standard size is called a bodyprint

These differences are called body shapes or simply shapes.

To draw your bodyprint you will need:

2¼ yards (2 m) of heavy-weight paper or Vilene or Pellon.

One black and one coloured ballpoint pen.

You can, if you wish, draw your bodyprint on a sheet of paper. But you are strongly recommended to draw it on Vilene.

The reason for using Vilene is that, unlike paper, it does not tear or crease. As you will be using your bodyprint for years to come, this is an important consideration.

To draw your bodyprint

Place the original basic pattern (which you bought) on the Vilene.

Draw around its edges with a ballpoint pen. Remove the pattern-pieces. Place the pieces of your toile on the corresponding outlines in the drawing.

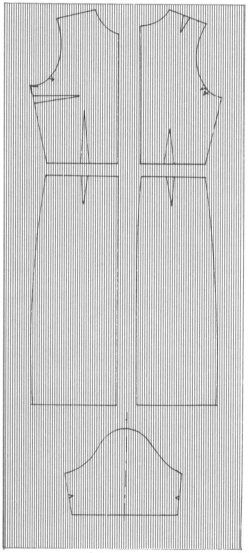

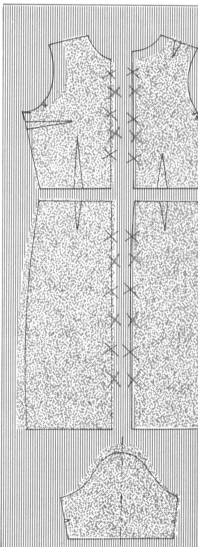

Make sure that the toile and the basic pattern coincide along the centre front and the centre back seams (indicated by XX in the illustration on the left).

This means that you cannot move the pieces of your toile sideways in relation to the basic pattern. But you can move them up and down to make them match the basic pattern drawn on the Vilene as closely as possible.

Here you have to use your common sense. To adjust a commercial dress pattern to your own measurements you will apply the shapes from the bodyprint on to the dress pattern. Clearly, therefore, you will want your shapes to be as few and as simple as possible.

When you are moving your toile pieces, always move the front and back of the bodice the same distance up or down.

This also applies to the front and back of the skirt.

Draw around each piece of the toile with a coloured ballpoint pen. When you have done this remove the toile pieces.

You now have your own bodyprint and can clearly see your shapes —the differences between your own and standard size measurements.

BODYPRINT

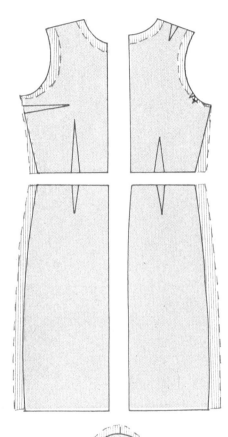

Guard your bodyprint jealously. It is an investment for a lifetime, and you may never need to make another one.

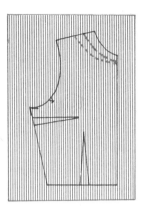

left side   — — —

right side   - - - - -

If you have differing measurements

If the measurements on one side of your body differ from those on the other:

First, draw your bodyprint as explained in this lesson, using only the left half of your toile.

Then place the pieces of the right-hand side of your toile on your bodyprint. Mark on the bodyprint the differences between your two sides (above).

To draw the bodyprint for your right-hand side, turn the pieces of the basic pattern over.
If there are a great many differences on a particular pattern-piece you may find it simpler to draw two bodyprints, that is, one for the left- and one for the right-hand side.

BODYPRINT

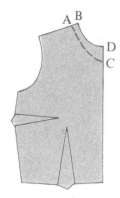

It has been stressed that to adjust a pattern to your own measurements all you have to do is apply to that pattern the differences between your own and standard measurements, that is, your shapes.

The following examples show how easy it is to use the formula for any style of pattern. The bodyprint has the basic round neckline and round armhole of your toile, but the same formula (joining A-C following the pattern outline) is applied first to a V-neck, second to a square armhole.

The formula

Measure A-B on your bodyprint.

Measure the same distance on the corresponding place on your pattern and mark Point A.

Measure C-D on your bodyprint.

Measure the same distance on the corresponding place on your pattern and mark Point C.

Join A to C on the pattern, following the pattern outline.

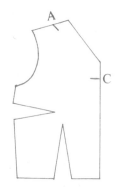

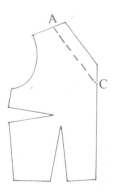

BODYPRINT

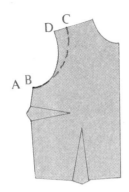

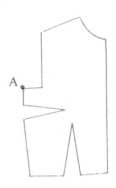

Measure A-B on your bodyprint.

Measure the same distance on the corresponding place on your pattern and mark Point A.

Rules

* A and C are always on the adjustment line, not on the pattern line.

* Every shape should be thought of as extending over the whole length of a particular seam line, even when part of it is on the seam itself.

* Some shapes are known as "plus shapes"—that is, you have to add them to your pattern.

* Other shapes are known as "minus shapes". These you have to take away from your pattern.

Measure C-D on your bodyprint.

Measure the same distance on the corresponding place on your pattern and mark Point C.

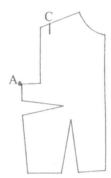

Join A to C on the pattern following the pattern outline.

It is essential to follow the outline of the pattern in order to keep the style the designer intended for the dress.

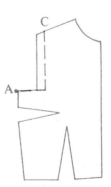

You now have your bodyprint and have learnt how to use it

The time has come to discover for yourself that dressmaking can be fun and successful every time.

First of all you will need to buy a dress pattern. Before you go out and buy one take a good look at your bodyprint. It can be your best guide when you are choosing your pattern. It will show you unmistakably which are the strengths and which are the weaknesses in your own figure.

As a general rule you should buy your pattern, material and all extras on the same shopping excursion. If you have to break this rule, make sure you buy your pattern before you buy your material.

Whenever you buy a dress pattern buy some heavy-weight "iron-on" Vilene to mount it on.

There are two reasons for this. Your pattern will be easier to handle; and if you want to enlarge the pattern you can do so on the surrounding Vilene.

Until you have become so familiar with this system that you can apply it almost automatically, keep the following summary beside you whenever you are adjusting a pattern to your own measurements.

1. On the dress pattern which you have bought, transfer all markings from the cutting line to the sewing line.

2. Cut out the pattern-pieces at the sewing line.

3. Mount the pattern-pieces on to "iron-on" Vilene. Leave a space of 4 inches (10 cm) between pattern-pieces. You will need this if you want to enlarge your pattern.

Place the Vilene with the pattern-pieces on it flat on your table. Put your bodyprint next to it.

4. With the help of the formula apply your shapes, one by one, to your pattern.

If you are in doubt check with the illustrations on pages 46 to 66.

5. You must apply every shape indicated on your bodyprint. You must not miss a single one. If you ignore this rule, your seams won't match, your dress won't hang right, and the result will be failure.

6. You must not make any alterations which are not indicated on your bodyprint. This rule is frequently ignored with results which are disastrous.

7. When you have applied all your shapes, make sure that all seams which have to be joined together are equal in length. If they are not, you must have made a mistake. Are you, for instance,

sure that the alteration you had to make was a plus, not a minus? Or a minus, not a plus?

8.   When you have adjusted all your pattern-pieces cut them out.

No matter what style of pattern you have chosen, you always apply the same shapes in the same way.

Every woman should have her own bodyprint

It will be useful even if you have no intention of making your own clothes but buy them ready-made.

A bodyprint will show you at a glance the differences between your own and standard measurements.

This will guide you in deciding which styles to buy and which to avoid.

It will show you what alterations are needed, and where, in the dresses you buy.

This will give you the confidence to tell a saleswoman or a dressmaker just what you need.

Different makes of pattern

Most British and American companies use the same standard measurements for their basic patterns.

So if you have used an American or British basic pattern for your bodyprint you will be able to use the patterns of any of the well-known American or British companies.

Companies on the continent of Europe, on the other hand, use different standard measurements. The illustration below shows the differences between an American or British basic pattern and a German one (shown by the pink dotted line).

These differences are quite easily resolved. If you have a bodyprint based on a British or American basic pattern and want to use, say, a German pattern made by Burda, buy the Burda basic pattern. Draw a second bodyprint using the Burda basic pattern and the pieces of your toile. Follow the instructions given on pages 40 and 41. It probably won't take you more than an hour or so.

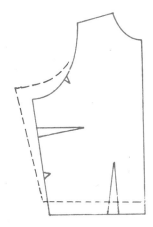

What if you lose your bodyprint?

If you lose your bodyprint, don't panic.

Provided you have kept both your basic pattern and the pieces of your toile, you should be able to draw a new bodyprint in a couple of hours.

If your figure changes

If your figure changes drastically, make a new toile.

It won't be necessary to go through the whole procedure again. You can trace the outline of your toile from your bodyprint and make it up in calico.

Try on your toile to see where it does not fit. The changes needed are unlikely to be alarming because, although you may have gained or lost weight, your bone structure and general proportions remain the same.

To make the alterations you need, see the illustrations on pages 28 to 37.

You can either make the alterations on your bodyprint or draw a new bodyprint.

On the following pages there are examples of many different styles, all of which can be easily adjusted when you follow the same simple formula.

Necklines

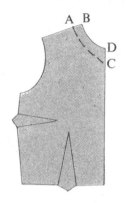

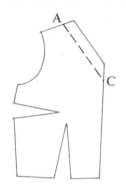

On the pattern to be adjusted:

Mark A

Mark C

Join A to C

Mark A

Mark C

Join A to C

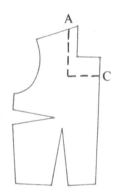

Mark A

Mark C

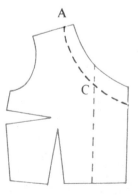

Remember that C-D is at the centre front of your bodyprint. In the case of a crossover pattern C must still be at the centre front.

Join A to C.

After joining A to C extend the alteration line to the edge of the pattern.

Armholes

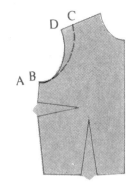

On the pattern to be adjusted:

Mark A

Mark C

Join A to C

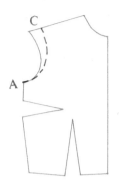

Mark A

Mark C

Join A to C

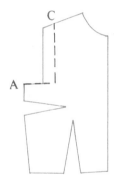

Mark A

Mark C

Join A to C

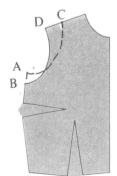

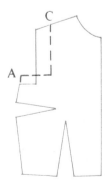

Shoulder seams

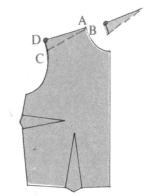

SHOULDER POINT •

You can, if you wish, follow the usual procedure, but there is a short cut.

With the help of tracing paper make a duplicate of the shoulder shape. Mark on it the alteration line and the shoulder point.

Example 1

Place the duplicate shoulder shape on the corresponding place on your pattern. Make sure that one shoulder point is on top of the other.

Mark A

Mark C

Remove the duplicate shape and pin it to the bodyprint for safe keeping.

Join A to C

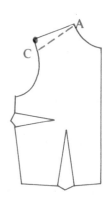

SHOULDER POINT •

48

BODYPRINT

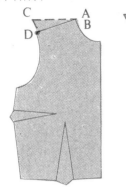

PATTERN TO BE ADJUSTED

Example 2

Place your duplicate shape on your pattern.

Mark A

Mark C

Remove your shape

Join A to C

Continue the alteration line to the end of the pattern. Extend the armhole tc meet the new shoulder line.

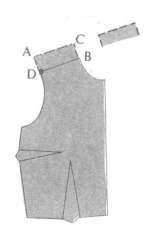

Example 3

Place your duplicate shape on your pattern.

Mark A

Mark C

Remove your shape

Join A to C
Extend the armhole and the neckline to meet the new shoulder line.

BODYPRINT

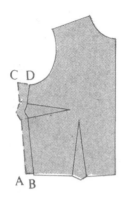

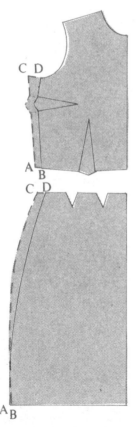

Side seams
Blouson-style bodice

On the pattern to be adjusted:

Mark A

Mark C

Join A to C

Dress without a waist seam

First adjust the side seam on the bodice of the pattern.

Mark A

Mark C

Join A to C

Next adjust the side seam on the skirt of pattern.

Mark A

Mark C

Join A to C

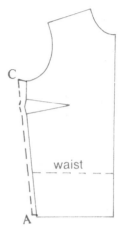

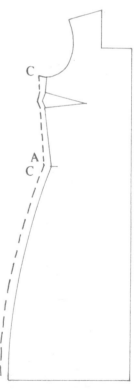

BODYPRINT

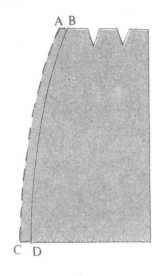

Skirt

On the pattern to be adjusted:

Mark A

Mark C

Join A to C

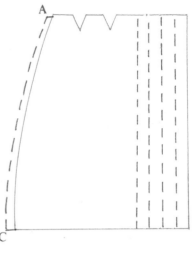

Mark A

Mark C

Join A to C

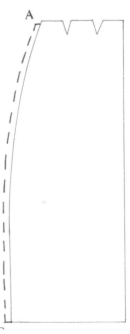

Waist seam

On the pattern to be adjusted:

Mark A

Mark C

Join A to C

Dress with a waist seam

This is simply a bodice and a skirt joined.

The rules for adjusting patterns for bodices and skirts apply.

On the bodice

Mark A

Mark C

Join A to C

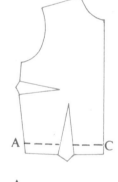

On the skirt

Mark A

Mark C

Join A to C

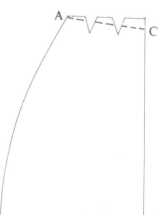

BODYPRINT

Dress without a waist seam

PATTERN TO BE ADJUSTED

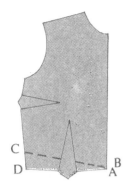

For a dress without a waist seam
you must apply only the shape
from the bodice of the bodyprint,
not the shape from the skirt.

Mark A

Mark C

Join A to C

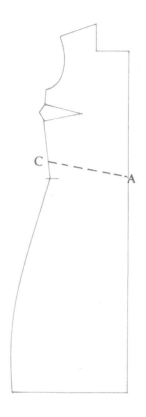

Sleeves

Mark A

Mark C

Join A to C

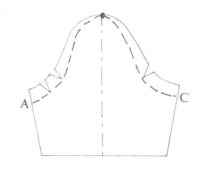

53

Yokes

A yoke is the top part of a bodice. It forms the shoulder seam and is part of both the neckline and the armhole.

On your work table place the pattern of the yoke and the pattern of the bodice together, as shown in the illustration on the right.

Treat the two pieces of pattern as one and apply your shapes in the usual way.

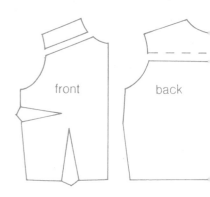

front   back

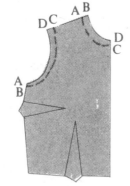

Example 1

On the armhole   **On the neckline**

Mark A   Mark A

Mark C   Mark C

Join A to C   Join A to C

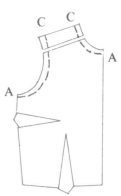

Example 2

On the yoke

Mark A

Mark C

Join A to C

In doing this you will have reduced the depth of the yoke and therefore altered the style of the dress.

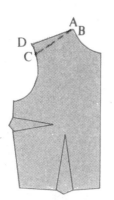

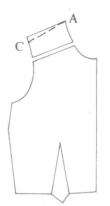

BODYPRINT

To restore the yoke to its original depth:

Add the amount you have taken off at the shoulder line to the bottom line of the yoke.

Then take off the same amount from the top of the bodice.

Yokes without shoulder seams

In these the front and the back of the yoke are cut from one pattern-piece.

Draw a line between the points indicating where the shoulder seam would be.

Cut the pattern along this line.

Place the pattern of the yoke front and the pattern of the bodice front together.

On the yoke front

Mark A

Mark C

Join A to C

Restore the yoke front to its original size.

Treat the back of the yoke in the same way.

Now rejoin the two parts of the yoke. Use sticky tape.

PATTERN TO BE ADJUSTED

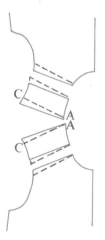

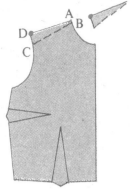

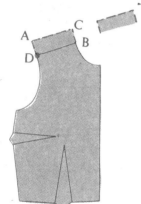

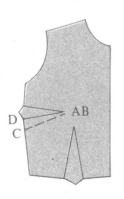

Kimono and dolman sleeves

Do not apply the armhole shapes. Use only your shoulder shapes (page 48).

Mark A

Mark C

Join A to C

Extend the alteration line to the end of the pattern.

Raglan sleeves

Do not make any alteration to the raglan line, and do not apply the armhole shapes. Apply your shoulder shapes (page 49).

Mark A

Mark C

Join A to C

Extend the alteration line to the end of the pattern.

In other respects apply normal procedures to dresses with raglan, kimono or dolman sleeves.

Darts

Example 1

Mark A

Mark C

Join A to C

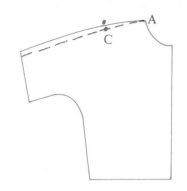

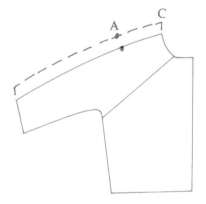

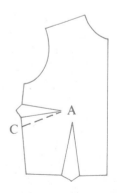

BODYPRINT

PATTERN TO BE ADJUSTED

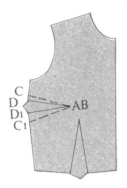

Example 2

Mark A

Mark C and C_1

Join A to C and to C_1

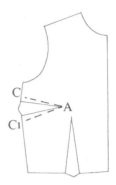

Note:
AB stands for the point of the dart shape on the bodyprint. It becomes a simple A on the pattern.

Example 3

Mark A

Mark C and C_1

Join A to C and to C_1

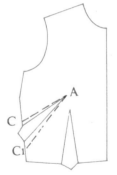

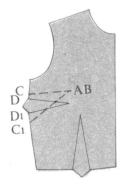

Example 4

Mark A

Mark C and C_1

Join A to C and to C_1

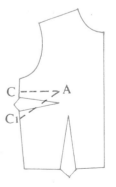

Patterns without darts

You will often find that your pattern does not have the same number of darts as your bodyprint. Some patterns have no darts at all. This means that the designer has incorporated the darts in some other way. In effect the darts are present but invisible.

Always follow the established rule; if your bodyprint shows any alterations to be made at any of the darts, apply these to your pattern.

To find where to place the dart shapes on your pattern

1. Measure on your bodyprint the distance between the top of the side seam and •.

Mark the same distance on your pattern.

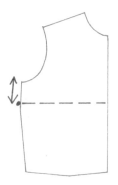

Draw a horizontal line from • across your pattern.

Measure on your bodyprint C-D and C_1-D_1.

Mark the same distances on your pattern, as shown in the illustration. Mark C and C_1.

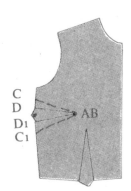

2. Measure on your bodyprint the distance between • and AB.

Mark the same distance on your pattern.

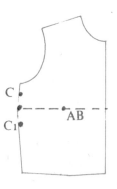

BODYPRINT

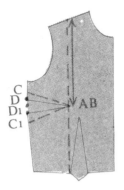

3.   Measure on your bodyprint the distance from the centre of the shoulder seam to point AB.

Mark the same distance on your pattern and mark A.

PATTERN TO BE ADJUSTED

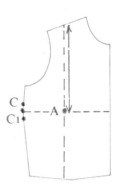

Join A to C and C_1.

Remember that you must apply only your shapes, and not the whole of the dart.

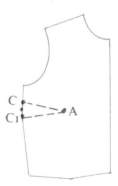

In some cases

Applying the shape in the corresponding place on the pattern would spoil the appearance of the dress.

The examples overleaf will show you how to avoid this!

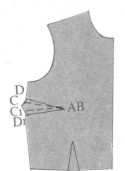

Bust dart to be made smaller

At the top of the side seam:

Mark A

Mark C

Join A to C

At the bottom of the side seam:

Mark A_1

Mark C_1

Join A_1 to C_1

Shoulder dart to be made smaller

Applying the shape to the corresponding place on the pattern would spoil the appearance of the dress. To avoid this, apply the shape to the armhole and to the neckline as shown in the illustration.

On the armhole:

Mark A

Mark C

Join A to C

On the neckline:

Mark A

Mark C

Join A to C

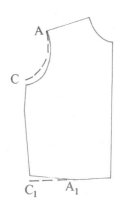

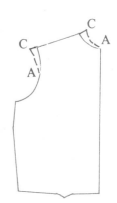

BODYPRINT

Waist dart to be made smaller

PATTERN TO BE ADJUSTED

Applying the shape to the corresponding place on the pattern would spoil the appearance of the dress. To avoid this, apply the shape to the side seam as shown in the illustration.

Mark A

Mark C_1 and C

Join A to C

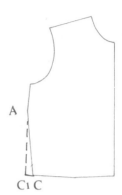

Waist dart to be made larger

Applying the shape to the corresponding place on the pattern would spoil the dress. To avoid this, apply the shape to the side seam as shown in the illustration.

Mark A

Mark C_1 and C

Join A to C

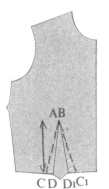

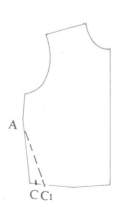

Belts

You can see on your bodyprint the difference between your own waistline and the standard size.

Let us suppose that your waistline is 1 inch (2 cm) larger than the standard.

For a straight belt

Divide the difference (1 inch / 2 cm) by 2. Add the result (½ inch / 1 cm) to each end of the belt.

For a curved belt

Divide the difference (1 inch / 2 cm) by 4, that is ¼ inch (5 mm).

Cut the belt pattern at the side markings (:).

Add ¼ inch (5 mm) to each cut end. Stick the pattern together again with sticky tape.

Interfacing

Cut your interfacing from your adjusted pattern-pieces.

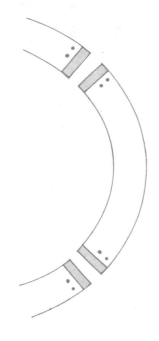
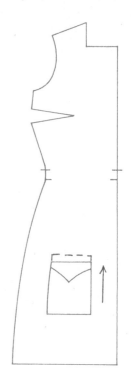

Pockets, flounces or embroidery on the skirt of a dress

On a dress with a waist seam

If you shorten or lengthen the bodice you will automatically bring the pockets, flounces or any other decoration on your skirt to the right position.

So there is no need for any other adjustment.

On a dress without a waist seam

In this case you will have to move pockets, flounces or other decorations up or down to the extent that you have shortened or lengthened the waist point on the dress.

Collars

Any adjustment made to the neckline has to be repeated on the collar.

You can alter collars by applying your shapes in the usual way. But there is also a short cut you can use.

Copy your collar pattern on to tracing paper.

Place the tracing paper on the adjusted dress pattern so that the neckline of the collar lies exactly on top of the original neckline of the dress pattern.

Keeping the tracing paper in this position trace the altered neckline. Making the adjustment you have just marked will alter the width of the collar and therefore change its style.

To put this right restore the collar to its original width. You do this by adding to the bottom of the collar the exact amount which you took off from the top.

Facings

Facings must be exact replicas of the corresponding pattern-pieces and cut on the same grain lines.

The easiest and quickest method is to cut out your facings from the adjusted pattern-pieces.

Apply every shape from your bodyprint on to your pattern. Take this instruction literally.

Do not leave out a single shape, and do not make any other alterations.

Start at the neckline and work downwards.

Adjusting a complete pattern

To adjust a whole pattern to your own measurements, copy each shape in turn from the bodyprint on to your pattern. You always use the same formula in exactly the same way. Start at the top and work downwards.

Check against the step-by-step instructions on pages 44-45 as you work.

YOUR PATTERN

BODYPRINT

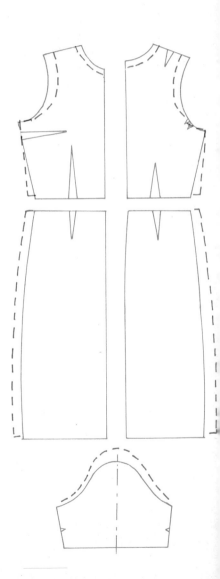

PATTERN TO BE ADJUSTED

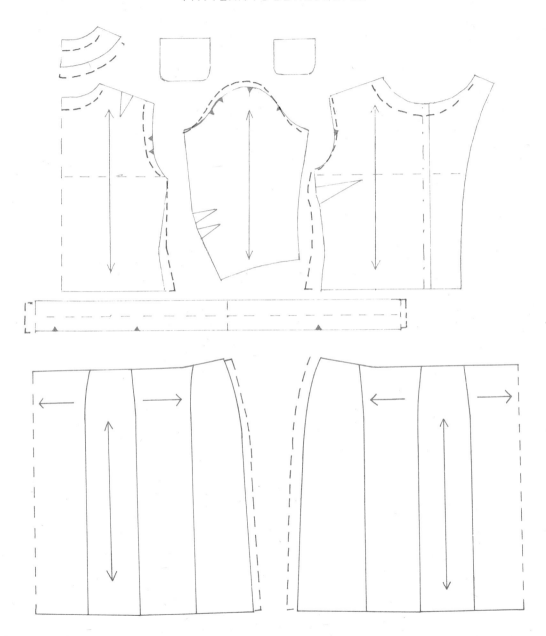

A complicated jacket adjustment, made easy

Here is a suit with a complicated jacket; using the same formula, the pattern is easily adjusted.

This example, and the one on the previous pages, show that the bodyprint can be used for any style and any part of a dress pattern.

If you are making something very different from your previous project, take the time to try out small details on scraps left over from the bodyprint calico, or left-overs from cutting out the dress.

For example, the suit pattern here has important buttonholes and buttons at the front of the jacket.

Always buy the buttons with the fabric, so you can see exactly how they will look and judge the size and effect accordingly.

There is no point in spending money on good fabric if you try to skimp on buttons and lining, or the fabric for the contrasting collar.

When you have finished the jacket remember to check the position of the buttonholes before you cut them into the material.

PATTERN TO BE ADJUSTED

It is essential to follow the method outlined in Part One in order to keep the proportions of the original design and ensure that the finished garment will look as though it was designed especially for you. All too often a garment made from a stunning pattern is ruined by poor fitting.

With your bodyprint, and the experience you will gain as you use it again and again, you will have the confidence to buy the most exclusive patterns and the best material you can afford.

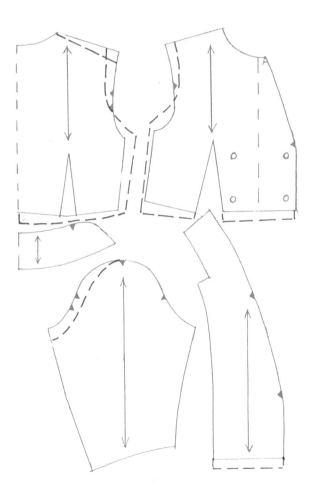

PART TWO

BASIC DRESSMAKING TECHNIQUES

The 24 lessons that follow illustrate the basic principles of dressmaking, with step-by-step instructions on how to apply them to a variety of different problems. They cover everything from preparing your pattern and fabric, to stitches, seams and darts, skirts, collars (simple and complicated) and finally buttonholes finished to haute couture standard.

How to read a pattern

Commercial patterns are normally sold in pattern envelopes. The information these envelopes contain and the style of presentation vary somewhat between different makes, but the following is an example of what you may find when you buy a pattern.

On the front of the envelope

The maker's name

The pattern number

The size

There is also a small sketch of the back of the dress.

If the pattern is a faithful copy of the work of a well-known designer this will be stated and the designer's name is given.

A photograph or an artist's impression of the dress. Sometimes you will find other sketches too. These (marked A, B, C, etc.) show variations on the original style. The pattern can also be applied to these variations.

On the back of the envelope

A detailed description of the dress

Tables showing the different sizes in which the pattern is available and the body measurements which correspond with these sizes.

Below these are shown the amounts of material needed for each pattern size.

The pattern envelope will quote different lengths of material for your dress, depending on whether you cut the material with or without nap.

Cutting "with nap"

Some fabrics such as velvet, imitation fur and corduroy have a pile or nap-finish to their surface. If you stroke them you will find your hand is going either with or against the pile.

If you hold the material with the pile going upwards it will, because of the way in which it reflects light, have a richer and deeper colour than if you hold it with the pile going downwards. A number of other materials with seemingly flat surfaces, such as satins and silks, have similar characteristics so far as reflecting the light is concerned.

With some materials the difference in shading may not be immediately visible. The danger here is that the difference may become apparent only after the dress has been made up—and ruined.

For this reason, it is advisable always to cut "with nap", that is with all pattern-pieces pointing in the same direction. If you cut "without nap" you may get a disastrous patchwork effect on your finished dress.

Inside the envelope

The layout plan. This shows you how to lay out your material and where to place the pattern-pieces. The information will be applicable to different bits of material and different pattern sizes.

The instructions. These are really a guide which shows you how to make up the dress.

The pattern. This consists of a number of pieces of paper on which the pattern-pieces are printed. On each of these are:

The pattern number

The size

A, B, etc., indicating the variations on the style (see front of envelope) to which the pattern-piece applies.

Instructions telling you how many times to cut out this pattern-piece. For example, you may have to cut out four pockets or two bodice fronts and only one bodice back.

There are also a number of symbols, illustrated on the right, on the pattern-pieces.

In the sewing instructions you will find frequent references to balance marks (top right). Broadly speaking, they are used as an aid to matching, or to indicate the beginning or the end of a stitching line.

Every balance mark has a counterpart on one of the other pattern-pieces. When pattern-pieces are joined balance marks must meet.

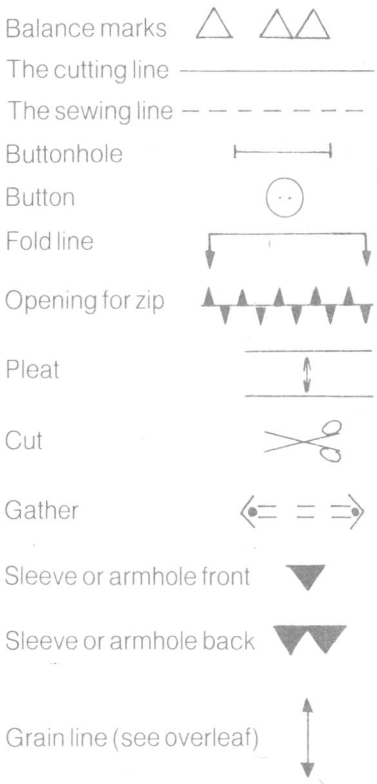

Balance marks	△ △△
The cutting line	——————
The sewing line	– – – – – –
Buttonhole	⊢————⊣
Button	⊙
Fold line	
Opening for zip	▼▲▼▲▼▲▼
Pleat	
Cut	✄
Gather	⟨•= = =⟩
Sleeve or armhole front	▼
Sleeve or armhole back	▼▼
Grain line (see overleaf)	↕

The importance of grain lines

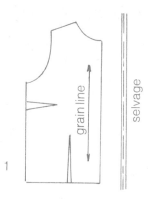

1

When you place the pattern-pieces on your material, always make sure the grain line on the pattern-piece lies exactly parallel with the selvage. "Selvage" is the name given to the thicker and firmer edge of the material. (1)

In the lengthways grain the fabric is stronger and less easily stretched. Materials have a natural tendency to hang in the direction of the lengthways grain. On the crossways grain the fabric stretches more easily. It will stretch more easily still if it is "on the bias", an imaginary line at 45° to both the lengthways and crossways grains. (2)

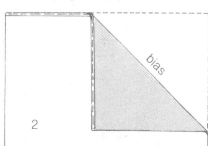

2

Garments must be cut on the lengthways grain.

Very occasionally for certain styles, part or all of the garment has to be cut on the bias or, on occasions, on the cross-grain.

Material which is "off the grain"

Sometimes in the manufacture of cloth the lengthways and crossways grains shift slightly in relation to each other. This produces what is known as material "off the grain".

The danger here is that you may not cut out your fabric on the true lengthways grain, with the result that your dress will not hang right.

In couture houses hours are sometimes spent in correcting a faulty grain. This can be done by steaming, pulling and ironing, but it is a specialist's job, and the amateur will probably make matters worse. Your safest course therefore is always to buy material which is "on the grain".

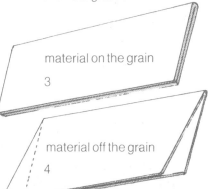

material on the grain

3

material off the grain

4

There is a simple way of testing whether material is in fact on the grain.

If you fold a piece of material in half, the two selvages and the two cut edges should meet exactly. If they don't the material is off the grain. (3) (4)

You can tolerate a discrepancy of up to about 1 inch (2 cm) but not more.

Do not confuse grain and grain line. Grain is the direction in which the thread which makes up the material runs. Grain line is a construction symbol which appears on patterns and must always run parallel with the selvage of the fabric.

Cutting on the right grain

Patterns are so designed that when you lay out your pattern-pieces the grain line must always run parallel with the selvage.

When no grain line is marked on the pattern-piece, it means that the centre front or centre back seams must run parallel with the selvage.

If you follow these rules you will automatically cut on the right grain. If you don't you will end up with the kind of result shown opposite.

Correct

The grain line on the pattern lies parallel with the selvage of the fabric.

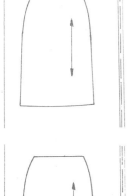

Incorrect

The grain line on the pattern does not lie parallel with the selvage of the fabric.

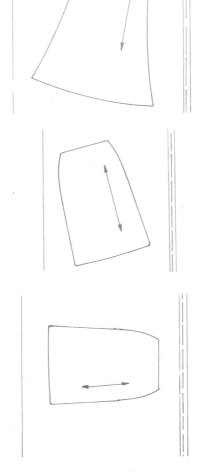

Result

The garment will not hang right.

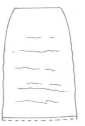

LESSON 2

Preparation of pattern and fabric

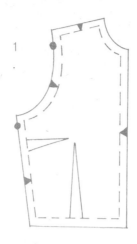

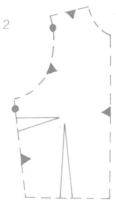

Select your pattern-pieces

The pattern you have bought may include a number of variations on the basic style. The pattern-pieces you select must of course all belong to the particular version you have chosen.

Cut out the pattern-pieces along the sewing lines

First transfer all markings from the cutting line to the sewing line. (1) (2)

Next cut out all the pattern-pieces along the sewing line.

This may seem strange to you, but there is a good reason for it.

The normal practice is to cut out the pattern-pieces along the cutting line.

As a result, when you place a pattern-piece on your fabric and draw around it, all you can mark on the fabric is the cutting line.

With our system, when you place a pattern-piece on your fabric and draw around it, you are marking the sewing line on your fabric.

You then measure on the fabric a distance of 1 inch (2 cm) all around on the outside of the sewing line and mark your cutting line there.

Having both your sewing line and the cutting line marked on your fabric will make your dressmaking much easier, quicker and more accurate.

Make your pattern easier to handle

Pattern-pieces are printed on flimsy tissue paper, which tears easily.

You can make them much easier to work with if you mount them on "iron-on" Vilene.

Iron-on Vilene is a man-made material with adhesive covering on one side.

On your ironing-board lay out the Vilene with the shiny adhesive side up.

Place the cut-out pattern-pieces with their printed side up on the Vilene.

With an electric iron press the pattern-pieces to the Vilene. (Use a fairly hot setting.) The heat will melt the adhesive and make the pattern stick to the Vilene.

Use only an up-and-down movement when you are pressing.

Do not slide the iron along the surface of the pattern.

Try not to get the adhesive on to your iron. If you do, clean it off immediately.

Cut out the pattern-pieces.

When you have done this, punch a hole in each of the pattern-pieces, thread a ribbon through it, and hang the pieces up ready to be used. (3)

You now have a pattern which you will be able to use with confidence.

The markings on the pattern are all clearly visible. It is firm and easy to work with.

Protect your fabric

Sooner or later every garment has to be cleaned. Clearly it will be heartbreaking if you make yourself a new dress and the first time it is cleaned it shrinks or the colours run. This can be avoided if you take certain precautions.

For dresses you intend to wash, before you cut into the material, always submit it to the washing process—by machine or by hand —which you intend to use later.

For dresses you intend to have dry-cleaned, there is no need to submit the fabric to any special process before you cut into it. If you are ironing such a dress, either when making it up or after it has been finished, do not use a damp cloth or steam.

The special case of wool

There is one exception to this rule. It concerns wool. You will probably want to have your woollen dresses dry-cleaned. When making a woollen dress, however, you will find that to get the seams to lie flat you have to iron them under a damp cloth. This will cause the material to shrink, and pucker, along the seam.

There are two ways of overcoming this difficulty.

You can take the material to the dry-cleaners and have it pre-shrunk before you cut into it. Or you can pre-shrink it yourself. (How to do this is explained in the next lesson, under "Pressing".) Once the material has been pre-shrunk you can damp press it.

The problem of finding the safest way to clean dresses has been simplified to some extent by manufacturers. Most materials are labelled with their contents and how they should be cleaned.

Working with different materials

Material	Before cutting	Finished garment
Cotton	Wash before cutting	Wash
Silk	—	Dry-clean
Wool	Pre-shrink before cutting, after which you can damp press	Dry-clean
Chiffon	—	Dry-clean
Velvet	—	Dry-clean
Lace embroidery	—	Dry-clean
Stretch fabrics in cotton	Wash before cutting	Wash
In silk	—	Dry-clean
Mixtures	If any of the fibres have to be dry-cleaned, you must dry-clean the whole fabric.	

Remember never to use a damp cloth or a steam iron on fabrics which need dry-cleaning.

Extras
Apply the same procedure to extras—lining, zip, interfacing, etc.—as you do to materials. In this way you can avoid having a well-made dress ruined by lining which has shrunk.

LESSON 3

Marking and cutting

Lay out your fabric

Use a cutting-board if you can (see page 125).

Always lay out your material with the reverse side up. Study the lay-out plan supplied with the pattern.

Unless the pattern instructions tell you otherwise, lay out your material lengthways and fold it in two so that the two selvages meet and lie parallel with the straight lines on your cutting-board. To hold the two layers together put a few pins both in the selvage and in the main body of the material.

Your material may at some point overlap your cutting-board. Either fold it at the end of the cutting-board or support it with a chair. It is important to prevent the material from stretching and pulling.

The selvage is sometimes firmer and thicker than the rest of the material and can, for this reason, prevent it from lying flat on the board. You can correct this by making small cuts, or nicks, diagonally into the selvage at intervals of 1 1/4 or 1 1/2 inches (3 or 4 cm).

Lay out your pattern

Lay the pattern-pieces on top of your material with the printed side up (unless your lay-out plan tells you otherwise).

Remember that your pattern-pieces are trimmed to the sewing line. To allow for seam allowances leave a space of 4 inches (10 cm) between pattern-pieces.

Remember how important it is to lay out your pattern-pieces so that they all point in the same direction —that is with nap (see page 68).

Keep the pattern-pieces in position with pins and weights.

Stick your pins straight down through pattern-pieces and material and into the cutting-board so that the pins remain upright. If you put the pins in sideways you will pick up and distort the material.

In addition to pins you should use weights to keep your pattern-pieces in position. You can, if you wish, use weights specially made for this purpose. Alternatively, you can use an ashtray or any other suitable object which happens to be handy.

Check the grain line. It was explained on page 70 that the

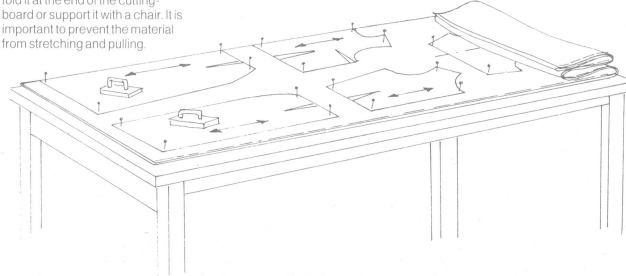

74

grain line on a pattern-piece must always lie parallel with the selvage of the material. To make sure, measure the distance between the grain line and the selvage at three or four points.

Make sure that you have enough material for all your pattern-pieces before you start cutting. Check that you have allowed for laying out the various pattern-pieces the necessary number of times. You may, for instance, need four pockets cut from one pattern-piece.

Mark the fabric

For marking use white or cream-coloured chalk. Make sure your chalk has a sharp edge.

When marking the material always use short strokes. Long strokes will drag the material and distort it. First mark along the sewing lines and balance marks.

Next copy all other markings from the pattern on to the material. These may include, for example, buttonholes, gathering lines, fold lines.

Now mark the cutting line all round the pattern-piece. This should be 1 inch (2 cm) from the sewing line.

Once you have finished marking, remove the weights which have been holding the pattern in place. Lift off the pattern very gently.

Pin the two layers of fabric together, placing the pins along the sewing lines and all markings. Pin at the corners. (1)

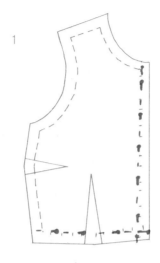

Pins   ●—►—►—►—

Sewing line   – – – –

Cut out the fabric

Cut out the material along the cutting line.

When cutting hold down the material with one hand and cut with the other. Make sure your scissors are supported by the cutting-board while you are cutting. If they are not, they may produce a dragging, distorting effect on the material.

Do not remove at this stage the pins which hold together the two layers of fabric.

Mark the lower layer of the fabric

Because you folded your material in two you will have cut out two layers of fabric for each pattern-piece, for example two sleeves, two fronts. But only the upper has been marked. To mark the lower layer:

Turn the two layers of material, which you have pinned together, over. Mark with chalk between the pins. Make sure you mark the corners accurately. Now you can remove all the pins and separate the two layers of fabric. (2)

Unless there is a seam, mark along the centre front and centre back of both bodice and skirt, and along the centre of the sleeve.

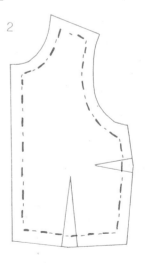

Pins   ●—►—►—►—

Sewing line – – – –

Stay-stitching

Stay-stitch along all sewing lines and other markings. A stay-stitch is a temporary stitch (page 74). Like all temporary stitches it should be sewn by hand, not by machine.

A stay-stitch will serve two purposes. It will prevent the material from stretching at the edge when you are working on it; and it acts as a sewing guide which is visible on both sides of the material.

Stay-stitch marginally on the seam allowance side of the sewing line, and use a contrasting colour thread. (1)

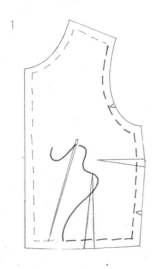

Sewing line — — —

Stay-stitch — — —

In all the lessons which follow, it will be assumed that you have cut, marked and stay-stitched your material as shown in this lesson. Instructions to do so will not therefore be repeated.

Notes:
Place the cut out and stay-stitched material in tissue paper and lay it flat. Put it carefully away.

Always complete the whole process of marking, cutting and stay-stitching one pattern-piece before starting on the next one. If you don't, you may be interrupted in your work, and when you pick it up again find that the two layers of material have shifted or the chalk marks have been erased. This can involve you in a lot of unnecessary work.

Don't handle your material more than you need to. You are making a new dress, but if you handle the material too vigorously it won't look new.

Once you have sewn up some of the seams, make a point of hanging up your dress when you are not working on it.

When hung it too should be covered with tissue paper.

Mark, cut and stay-stitch extras such as lining, interfacing. Follow the same procedures as for the main material.

At this stage you may feel that it has taken you rather a long time to cut and mark.

This may be so. But it is not time wasted.

Remember that you will be working with a perfectly adjusted pattern. With this and material which has been carefully cut and marked, you will probably be surprised by the speed with which you progress from now on and more than pleased with the accuracy of the result. Never begrudge time spent on preparation.

Working with different fabrics

If you are working with slippery materials or those which stretch very easily (for example silk chiffon or silk jersey) you will find the easiest way to cut your fabric is as follows:

With the right sides together fold your fabric in two.

On your left-hand side pin the short ends of the fabric to the table (you need a cutting-board for this).

Smooth out the fabric very carefully and pin the two layers together at the selvages.

Lay out your pattern and from then on follow the standard procedure.

Working with patterned fabrics

Making up a dress from a patterned material can present you with certain problems. Generally speaking, the larger the design the bigger the problem.

For one thing a large design—a flower for example—must appear on the correct part of the dress. And whatever the design, it must match where it has been cut and joined. (3)

In a dress these points may be: centre front and centre back seams, side seams, sleeves, any other vertical or horizontal seams and at the hemline (if your fabric has a crossways design).

Fabric with a crossways design

If a fabric has the design running across it you should start matching at the hemline and work upwards.

At the side seams you will find that if you have a dart in front, you cannot match the fabric between the bust dart and the armhole. This is unavoidable. (2)

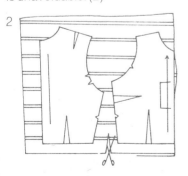

Laying out patterned material

Lay out your fabric lengthways and fold it in two. The fold of the material must follow the straight lines of the design. Pin the two layers of fabric together so that identical patterns lie one on top of the other. (4)

With some designs this will be impossible to do. In such cases lay out your fabric in a single layer.

Laying out your pattern

Lay your pattern-pieces on your material in such a way that the design of the material matches at corresponding balance marks. The matching at the balance marks must take place at the sewing line, not the cutting line. (5)

The reason for this is that you see in the made-up dress what appears at the sewing line. So every time you make a seam you must to some extent break the pattern. If your fabric has a large design, use it for a dress with a minimum of seams.

Note:
Your dress will have two sleeves, and the front of the dress may be cut from two pattern-pieces. When you are cutting out from a single layer of fabric remember to turn your pattern paper over before cutting the second piece. Otherwise you will cut yourself two left sleeves or two right fronts.

3

4
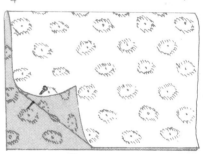

5
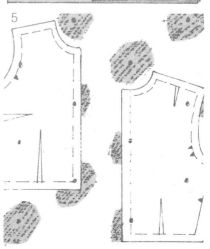

LESSON 4

Sewing stitches

When you are making up a garment you are either sewing by hand or stitching by machine. When stitching you should follow the instructions which are included with your sewing machine.

The advice in this lesson is intended to help you when hand-sewing.

Left-handed dressmakers can work from left to right instead of from right to left.

The stitches used in hand-sewing are of two main kinds, the temporary and the permanent.

Temporary sewing stitches

All temporary stitches should be done by hand.

A temporary stitch should be longer than those used in ordinary sewing. The additional length will make the stitch easier to remove.

The length of the stitch should depend on the type of fabric for which it is needed. The heavier the fabric the longer the stitch.

Running stitch

Weave the needle in and out through the fabric before finally pulling it through. This can be used for tacking or stay-stitching. (1)

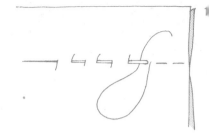

Permanent sewing stitches

Oversewing

This is used for oversewing cut edges by hand. (2)

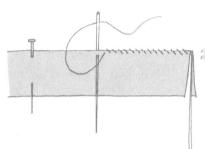

Invisible stitch

This is commonly used for joining two pieces of material, for example a hem to a skirt. (3)

One advantage of this method is that when you have finished sewing the stitch is almost invisible.

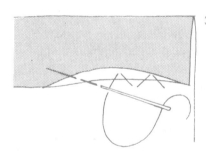

Back-stitch

Insert the needle just behind the point where you last took it out, and then take it out again just beyond that point. (4)

The result is a firm stitch which can, if needed, replace machine stitching.

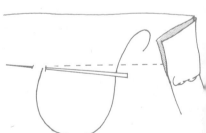

Slip-stitch

This is used for joining two pieces of fabric together. Slide the needle along the edge of the fold, then diagonally across to the main fabric and pick up a few threads. (5)

Prick-stitch

This is a variation of the back-stitch, the difference being that the stitch is so short it is barely visible on the right side of the material. Prick-stitching is commonly used for inserting zips. (6)

Cross-stitch

(Your needle picks up only the top layer of fabric.)

Unlike the other stitches so far described, this is worked from left to right—if you are right-handed. (7)

Blanket-stitch

Insert the needle about 1/4 inch (5 mm) from the edge of the fabric. Bring the needle out underneath the material to the outside edge with the thread behind the needle. Continue working from left to right at 1/4 inch (5 mm) intervals. (8)

A variant on this, with the needle inserted at intervals of about 1/16 inch (1 mm), is used for covering hooks and bars and belt carriers.

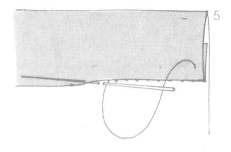

5

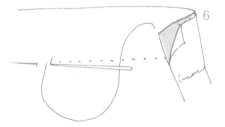

6

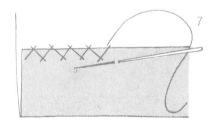

7

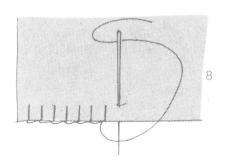

8

Guide to buying sewing thread

There are four main types of sewing thread available: cotton, silk, man-made and multipurpose.

Cotton thread is used for cotton and other natural fabrics.

Silk thread is used for silk and wool. It is becoming increasingly hard to obtain. As a substitute you can use multipurpose thread.

Man-made thread is used for man-made fabrics. This type of thread has a built-in stretch quality and should be used for all stretch fabrics.

Multipurpose thread combines the qualities of cotton and man-made threads. It is designed to suit all materials, including stretch fabrics.

For temporary stitches use **tacking thread**, which is specially manufactured for this purpose.

It is cheaper than ordinary thread and stays in position more easily.

Ironing and pressing

There is a difference between ironing and pressing.

Ironing

Ironing eliminates crease-marks from the material. In ironing, the iron remains in contact with the surface of the material as you slide the iron to and fro.

Pressing

Pressing helps to give a garment its shape. When pressing, the iron is lifted and pressed down.

Both ironing and pressing should always be done on the reverse side of the fabric. Remember also to remove all tacking and pins before ironing or pressing. If you don't, they may leave marks. Ironing and pressing are often a combined operation. This operation will be referred to simply as "pressing" from here onwards.

You should always press a garment, or part of a garment, in the direction of the lengthways grain. This is particularly important to remember when you are pressing curved seams or material cut on the bias.

If you don't follow this rule you will stretch your fabric out of shape.

The right temperature for your iron

Read the manufacturer's instruction book and follow the guidance marked on your iron.

Some fabrics, such as silk, can easily be ruined by too hot an iron even if they haven't been burned. The silk can become stiff and also lose its sheen.

Pressing on a flat or curved surface

Most of your pressing should be done on an ironing-board. But any curved part of the garment such as darts, curved seams or arm-holes, must be pressed over a curved surface such as a tailor's ham. (1)

Pressing dry or with steam

You will find with some materials you won't be able to get rid of creases or set the shape of the dress correctly unless you press it "damp".

You can do this either by using a steam iron or by using an ordinary iron and a damp cloth.

To steam-press with an ordinary iron, place a bowl of lukewarm water and two or three ironing-cloths next to your ironing-board. Make sure that your ironing-cloth is only very slightly damp. You may find it helpful to have several

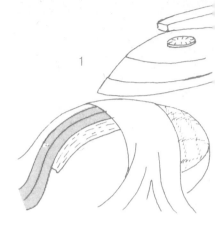

damp cloths and to use one while the others dry off a little. For information on ironing-cloths see page 126.

Always let the material dry off before handling it again. If you don't, you will create new creases.

Shrinking

In dressmaking it is sometimes necessary to shrink the whole or part of a fabric. For example, you may want to pre-shrink a woollen fabric before cutting into it.

To shrink a fabric you simply damp press all over.

To make sure that the fabric shrinks evenly, slide the iron so that it barely touches the fabric. The steam generated in this way will move freely and will be evenly distributed over the fabric. Pressing plays a very important part in dressmaking. You will learn more about it under various headings in this book.

Working with different fabrics

Chiffon. This has a very fine, slightly uneven surface and can be stretched easily.

To guard against this, press very lightly and never with steam or a damp cloth.

Velvet and other pile fabrics. Velvets have a pile finish, which should not be flattened.

To guard against this, take a spare piece of your velvet fabric and place it right side up on your ironing-board. With the right sides together place your main fabric on top of this spare piece. Place your ironing-cloth on top and press.

The bottom layer of velvet, the spare piece, will act as a cushion and prevent the main piece from being flattened. Alternatively, you can use a velvet board.

Embroidery and lace. The pattern, or design, in lace or embroidery is liable to be slightly higher than the level of the rest of the material. This too should not be flattened.

Fold a towel three or four times and place it on your ironing-board. Place the lace or embroidery face downwards on the towel. Press lightly.

Stretch fabrics. Always press dry.

Remember never to damp press a fabric which is intended to be dry-cleaned only.

Do not damp press wool unless it has been pre-shrunk.

Always test a small piece of your fabric before starting to press the whole garment.

Use strips of brown paper when pressing seams or darts.

For all equipment used in ironing and pressing see pages 125 and 126.

LESSON 6

Seams

> When you are dressmaking do not put your material on your lap or hold it in mid-air. Make sure that it rests firmly on a table.

Whenever you join two pieces of material together you create a seam.

Seams can be straight, curved or enclosed.

For any kind of seam you should follow the five main steps in sewing.

These are:

Pin

Tack

Stitch

Press

Trim

Straight seams

Pin

When pinning together two pieces of material, make sure that the sewing line of one is exactly on top of the sewing line of the other. Pin through both layers of material with the pins lying lengthways along the sewing line. (1)

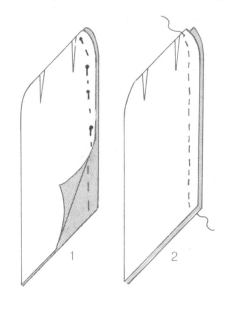

Tack

Tacking is a temporary joining of two pieces of material. It is done by hand. (For tacking stitches see page 78.)

When you are tacking, stop whenever you reach a corner, cut the thread and start again. The reason for this is that you will want to remove parts of the temporary stitches at different times while you are making a dress. If the sewing is all on one thread, it will crumple the material when you pull it out and you may pull out more than you intend to. (2)

Stitch

Stitching is sewing by machine. To make sure you have the right type and length of stitch, experiment with a small piece of your material.

The stitch, as seen on the right side of the material, should be smooth and firm and should not pucker. There should be no large gap between stitches. You may have to try various stitch lengths before you get the right result. Study the manufacturer's instructions carefully.

The bulk of the material which you are working on should lie to the left-hand side of the foot of the sewing machine. Hold and guide your material with both hands when stitching. One hand should be behind the needle and one in front. (3)

When you have finished stitching, remove the tacking threads.

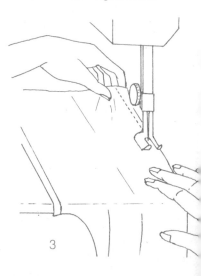

Press

Stitching and pressing should be regarded as part of the same process. Every time you stitch you must immediately press. This is an important rule of dressmaking. Observing it will make a great deal of difference to the finished dress.

Remember to press only on the reverse side of your fabric.

Pressing a seam

A.   Set your stitches.

Turn both seam allowances in the same direction and press over the stitching line. This will cause the stitches to sink into the fabric. (4)

B.   Press the seam open.

To prevent any impression made by the seam allowance from showing on the right side of the material, place a strip of brown paper between the seam allowance and the garment while pressing. (5)

Trimming and layering

When you have finished stitching a seam you will often find that you are left with too much seam allowance. This creates unnecessary bulk. To reduce the bulk trim the seam allowances, leaving about ¾ inch (2 cm).

In most dresses seam allowances will be pressed open. But in some cases, for example at a yoke or a gathering, both seam allowances will be pressed to the same side.

Pressing them to the same side causes additional bulk. You can reduce the bulk by trimming one seam allowance shorter than the other. This process is known as "layering". (6)

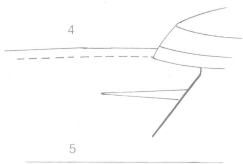

4

5

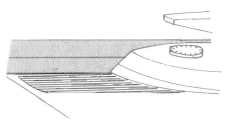

6

Preventing seams from stretching or breaking

It is important to prevent your seam from breaking or being stretched at points where there is additional strain, for instance at shoulder seams, waist seams and some necklines.

Buy a length of tape about ½ inch (1.5 cm) wide. Use your pattern, not your dress, as a guide and cut the tape to the same length as the seam you want to reinforce. This will ensure that you have the correct length. Centre the tape over the sewing line of the seam and attach it by hand through the stitching line. Ease the fabric on to the tape. (7)

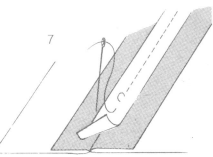

7

Curved seams

On a straight seam the strain is evenly distributed. On a curved seam the strain is greater at the curve. Consequently garments tend to tear more easily at the curve than anywhere else on the seam.

To prevent this happening you should reinforce the curved part of the seam with a "guard-line". A guard-line is an extra row of stitches in the seam allowance running $\frac{1}{8}$ inch (2 mm) from the sewing line. Guard-lines must be stitched into both pieces of material before you sew them together. (1)

When you have finished stitching the guard-lines, join the two pieces of fabric together. (2)

From here on follow the same procedure as for straight seams.

Pin, tack, stitch. When stitching, stretch the fabric gently to prevent the seam from puckering.

Press. Again stretch the fabric gently, and snip into the seam allowances to make them lie flat.

All curved seams should be pressed over a curved surface, such as a tailor's ham. (3)

Trim. Trim close to the guard-line. Be careful not to cut into the guard-line.

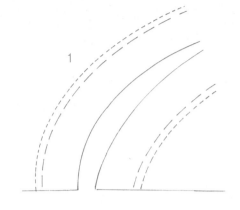

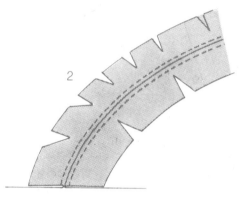

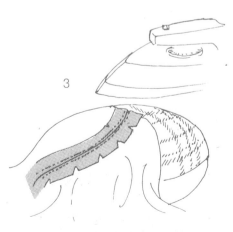

Enclosed seams

Enclosed seams are to be found in waistbands, cuffs and collars.

It is very important that when the dress is finished there should be clean, well-defined edges at these points.

To achieve this, when you have sewn up the collar (or cuff or waistband) turn it inside out. The two right sides will now be facing each other.

Set the stitches. Press the seams open.

If you now look at the right side you will find that you have a clean edge along the sewing line.

Trim as close as you can to the sewing line $\frac{1}{8}$ inch (2 mm) and diagonally across at the corners. (4

Turn the fabric to the right side. If necessary pull the corners out with a pin. Never push from the inside with scissors.

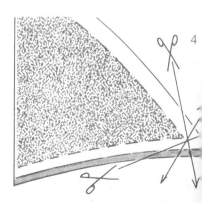

Working with different fabrics

If you are working with a fabric which slips easily, such as chiffon or georgette, place a layer of white tissue paper underneath the two layers of fabric. Stitch through both layers of fabric and the paper.

When you have finished stitching, pull the tissue paper away.

Stretch fabrics

Use ballpoint needles on your machine. The blunt point at the tip of the needle will prevent it from catching in the fabric. Buy special sewing thread which has an elastic quality. (For notes on threads see page 79). Ordinary thread is liable to break when the seam stretches.

As you stitch, stretch the fabric to prevent seams from puckering. You may find it a wise precaution to have a trial run with a small piece of the fabric and to try stretching it after you have done some stitching. If the stitches snap or the material puckers, use a longer stitch and stretch the fabric slightly more while you are stitching.

Machine with a straight stitch, unless your machine has a special stitch for stretch fabrics.

Lace

The perfect lace dress has no seams. There is only one way to achieve this. Where joining has to be done, do not stitch but, instead, appliqué (embroider) pieces of lace together so that the design on the lace remains intact.

Guide to tapes

For **medium- and heavyweight fabrics** use organza strips, preferably the selvage of the organza, or $1/4$ - $1/2$ inch (5 mm - 1 cm) wide cotton tape.

For **lightweight fabrics** use organza or the selvage of the same fabric.

For **transparent fabrics** use organza.

For **cottons** use cotton organza, for **silks**, silk organza, and for **man-made fabrics**, man-made organza.

Joining different materials

If you are joining two different materials—such as velvet and taffeta—place the more difficult one to work with, in this case the velvet, on top. You will see more clearly what you are doing.

Similarly, if you have to join a gathered or pleated fabric to a straight fabric, always place the more difficult piece to deal with—in this case the one which has been gathered or pleated—on top.

LESSON 7

Darts

In this lesson you will learn about different darts:

Straight (standard) dart

Curved dart

Open dart

Trimmed dart

The choice of dart will depend on the type of material used.

Straight dart

For light- and mediumweight fabrics

Pin together at the sewing lines. Start in the seam allowance 1/4 inch (5 mm) from the sewing line. Always start at the widest part and work towards the narrowest—to the point of the dart. (1)

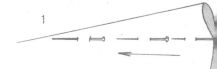

Tack. Again start at the widest part and work towards the narrowest. (2)

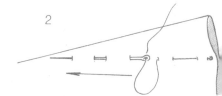

Stitch. Again work from the widest to the narrowest part. When stitching do not stop the machine when you reach the point of the dart: carry on for a few more stitches even if you feel you are machining in mid-air. The purpose of this is to give the completed dart a smooth, tapered finish. Do not back-stitch at the point of the dart. To finish the stitching line tie a knot from the two loose ends of the thread and, using a sewing needle, work these ends into the stitching line. Back-stitching would create a lump which would be visible in the garment. (3)

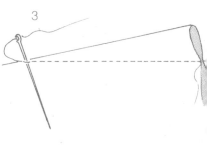

Curved dart

Follow the procedure for a straight dart, but be careful to get a smooth, tapering finish at the points. Don't back-stitch at either end. Snip into the dart to make it lie flat. (4)

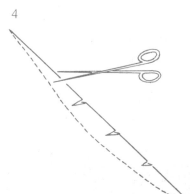

Pressing

Press darts on a curved surface—such as a tailor's ham. Remember to use a strip of brown paper between the fabric and the dart. (5)

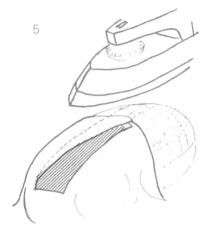

5

Always press vertical darts away from the centre front or centre back, and horizontal darts downwards. (6)

No trimming is needed for straight darts.

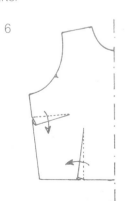

6

Open dart

For bulky fabrics

When you make a standard dart you end up with three layers of material. This is perfectly satisfactory for light- or medium weight fabrics. But in heavy weight fabrics, such as tweeds, it would create too much bulk.

A variation on the standard dart which will serve to reduce bulk is the open dart.

First pin, tack, stitch and press as for a straight dart. Then slit the dart open as far as you can. Then snip sideways to make the fabric lie flat.

Press the dart open on a curved surface. Press to one side the part of the dart which was too small to slit open.

There is no need to trim the dart. Oversew the cut edges by hand. (7)

Trimmed dart

For transparent or very light fabrics

A dart showing through a transparent fabric can be very unattractive. To avoid this:

First pin, tack and stitch as a straight dart. Then stitch a guardline in the body of the dart $\frac{1}{8}$ inch (2 mm) from the stitching line.

Press using a tailor's ham.

Remember to use strips of brown paper.

Trim the dart close to the guardline, oversewing the raw edge by hand. (8)

Notes:
Whenever practicable use the straight dart.

Once a dart is opened or trimmed it cannot be altered.

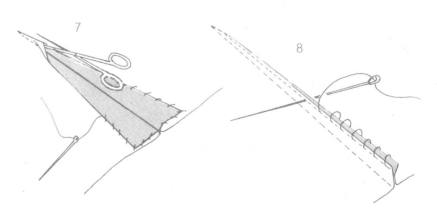

7

8

LESSON 8

Gathering

To produce a pleasing appearance gathering should:
Be evenly distributed
Not form pleats
Hang straight

On your dress pattern the marks for gathering are two broken lines placed in the seam allowance and running parallel to each other. The beginning and the end of the gathering lines are marked.

Gathering should always be done by machine and not by hand.
Do not gather across a seam line. Stop stitching before you reach the seam. Cut the thread and start again.

To find the correct stitch-length for gathering the fabric you are working on:

Take a spare piece of the dress material and, on the right side of the fabric, stitch two rows along it ⅛ inch (2 mm) from each other and about 6 inches (15 cm) in length.

Turn the fabric to the reverse side. Gather up the fabric by pulling up both gathering threads at the same time. Do one side at a time.

If the gathering is firm enough not to slide about, but at the same time allows you to redistribute the fullness without breaking the thread, your stitch-length is right. If not, try again with a different length until you get the result you want.

For gathering you will find that you need a fairly strong thread.

Do not gather more than 18 inches (50 cm) at a time. If you do, your thread may break.

Having found the correct stitch-length and thread, you can now start work on your dress material.

On the right (not, as normally, the reverse) side of the material stitch along the two gathering lines:
<•===•>.

Place in front of you the piece of material with the gathering lines and the piece of material it has to be attached to. (1)

Pin the two pieces of material together at the centre and at the two ends of the gathering lines. Always work with the material to be gathered lying on top.

Starting on the left half, pull up both gathering threads at the same time until the two pieces of material have become the same length.

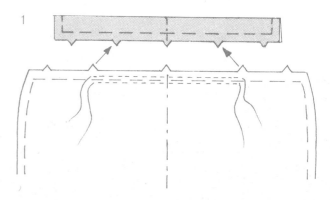

Secure the threads by winding them round a pin in a figure of 8. (2)

Repeat the procedure for the right half.

Match the rest of the balance marks, and pin. Place the pins at right angles to the sewing lines. Check that the sewing lines overlap.

Remove the pins.

Stitch. When stitching hold and guide the material so that gathers remain at right angles to the stitching line.

Press. Turn both seam allowances

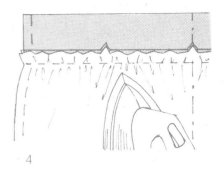

4

2

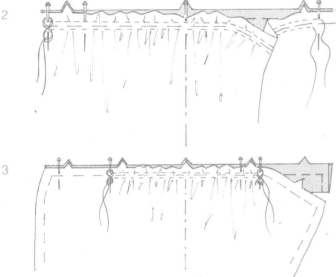

3

Distribute the gathers evenly between the balance marks with the point of a pin. Keep the gathers in position with additional pins placed at right angles to the sewing line. (3)

Tack the two pieces of the material together at the sewing line. Use small stitches.

in the same direction, away from the gathering. Press the gathers with the tip of the iron only. (4)

Trim and layer. The seam allowance of the gathered material should become the shorter of the two.

With material which frays, oversew the cut edges by hand.

Easing

In this book and elsewhere, when you read about dressmaking, you will come across the term "easing".

"Easing" is something you may have to do when you join two pieces of material, one of which is slightly (up to perhaps ¾ inch/2 cm) wider or longer than the other. Thus you may be told to ease your skirt on to your bodice, the skirt being slightly the wider of the two. Similarly, when a shoulder seam has stretched and you want to make it the same length as a tape you are attaching it to, you do this by easing.

Easing is really gathering on a small scale.

To ease, you make a double row of gathering stitches on the right side of the material. Pull up the gathering thread and distribute the fullness evenly. Then pin, tack and stitch as in gathering.

Interfacing

Interfacing serves to give extra body to a fabric.

It is used chiefly for collars, cuffs, pockets, belts, buttonholes and front openings.

Material for interfacing

There are two main kinds of interfacing: sew-on and iron-on.

Sew-on interfacing
Interfacing of this kind is sewn to the main material by hand.

Iron-on interfacing
This interfacing has adhesive on one side and is joined to the main material by ironing.

What happens is that the heat of the iron melts the adhesive and this causes the two fabrics to stick to each other.

Cutting out interfacing

To cut out either kind of interfacing you should use the same pattern-pieces as for the main material.

Cut out the interfacing along the sewing line, not the cutting line. In effect this means leaving no seam allowance. (1)

Attaching interfacing to the main material

Sew-on interfacing

Lay out the pieces of material you want to interface with the reverse side up. (2)

Place the interfacing on the main material, with the two reverse sides together.

Attach the interfacing to the main material at the sewing line. Sew by hand. (3)

Iron-on interfacing

Lay out and cut as for sew-on interfacing. The reverse side is the one with the adhesive and the shinier surface.

Attach by pressing, that is with an up-and-down movement of the iron.

Do not slide your iron along the material. Your iron should be at the right temperature for the fabric. (See the instructions on the iron.)

If you get any adhesive on your iron, clean it off immediately.

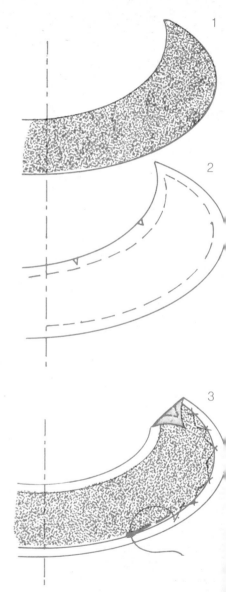

Guide to materials for interfacing

Vilene

This is a non-woven, man-made fabric. It has no grain line and can be cut in any direction.

Vilene is manufactured in a wide range of different weights, making it suitable as an interfacing for most fabrics. It is either black or white.

There are two forms of Vilene, "sew-on" and "iron-on". The manufacturer's instructions should guide you in your choice between the two.

In couture houses the following fabrics are also commonly used for interfacing:

Material	Interfacing
Fine cotton	Victoria lawn or cotton organdie
Silk	Silk organza or silk taffeta
Wool	Cotton
Very fine wool	Organza
Man-made silk fabrics	Polyester
Nylon velvet	Polyester organza
Cotton velvet	Victoria lawn
Lace	Fine nylon net
Transparent natural fabrics	Silk organza in a matching colour
Transparent man-made fabrics	Polyester organza in a matching colour
General use	Cotton Moycell, a natural fabric, available in iron-on form

Notes:

You can usually buy interfacing in the material or haberdashery department of a store.

When choosing your interfacing, hold a piece of the main material and the interfacing together to test whether the interfacing provides the right degree of firmness.

Like all extras your interfacing must complement your main material.

In particular it must react to washing (or other forms of cleaning) in the same way as the main material does.

It is important to remember that iron-on interfacing will be firmer after you have attached it to the fabric.

LESSON 10

Finishing

The purpose of finishing seam allowances is not only to produce a more pleasing appearance. It also prevents the material from fraying.

There are a number of ways of finishing a seam. But they are all based on one or other of the following techniques:

Top-stitching

Oversewing by hand

Turning the cut edge under

Applying a facing to the cut edge

Enclosing the cut edge between two layers of material

Your choice of technique will depend on the type of fabric you are working on.

Light- or mediumweight fabrics which hardly fray

You can stitch a guard-line ¼ inch (5 mm) from the edge of the seam allowance. Or you can oversew by hand or overlock by machine. (1)

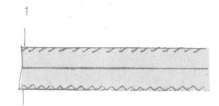

Light- or mediumweight fabrics which fray badly

You can turn the cut edge under and stitch by machine. Be careful not to stretch the edge of the fabric. (2)

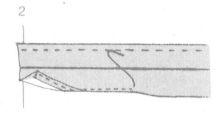

Heavy and bulky fabrics

For all heavy and bulky fabrics oversew the cut edges by hand. Alternatively enclose the cut edge between two layers of fabric.

For this you need a bias binding, which you can buy in a shop or make yourself. A bias binding is a strip of material in which the two long edges have been turned under. The folds produced may be the same width, or one may be narrower than the other. (3)

The bias bindings you can buy are normally made of cotton or satin in a large range of colours and in different widths.

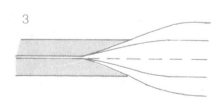

Apply a bias binding to your seam

Open out one fold of the binding. With the right sides together, pin the upper fold line of the binding

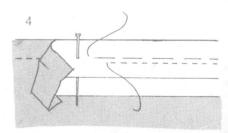

on top of the sewing line of the fabric. Tack and stitch. (4)

Trim the seam allowance to a width slightly narrower than the fold in the binding.

Finish. Fold the binding over to enclose the raw edges. Attach the free edge of the binding to the reverse side of the material by hand, using a slip-stitch. (5)

Making your own bias binding

A number of times in dressmaking you may find it necessary to make up your own bias binding.

Place your material with the right side up and fold it so that the selvage and one crossways edge meet. (6)

Using an electric iron, press your fold line, which is the true bias.

Open out the fold line and mark along it with tailor's chalk. Then draw a line parallel to the fold line.

The width of the strip made by this line should be four times the required width of the finished binding plus 1/4 inch (5 mm), depending on the thickness of the fabric. (7)

Mark within the strip two fold lines parallel with the long ends of the strip.

Each fold should be one-quarter of the total width.

Mark in the same way as many bias strips as you require.

Cut out the strips.

To join the bias strips: mark sewing lines at each of the narrow ends of the strips 1/2 inch (1 cm) from the edges.

With the right sides together, pin the bias strips together so that the sewing lines match exactly. You will find that your cutting lines will not match. Don't worry about this.

Pin, tack, stitch, press the seam open and trim the seams. (8) (9)

To finish your bias binding turn the binding over lengthways at the fold lines and press.

Using bias binding is one of the most important techniques in dressmaking. As you progress through this book you will discover that waistbands, cuffs and most types of collar are based on the same principle as bias binding.

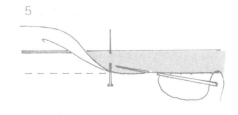

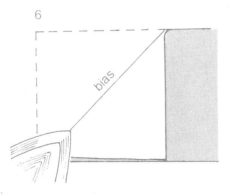

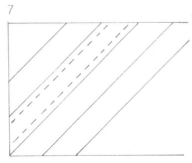

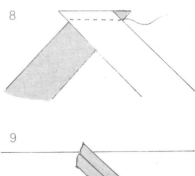

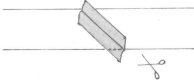

Very light fabrics

French Seam

This type of seam is only for very fine fabrics and straight seams.

Its main advantage is that the seam is joined and finished in a single operation.

To make up a French seam

Draw a chalk line ¼ inch (5 mm) from the sewing line in each seam allowance.

With the reverse sides facing each other, pin the two pieces of fabric together along the lines you have just drawn. (1)

Tack, stitch, and press the seam open.

Press again, turning both seam allowances to the same side.

Trim the seam allowance to ⅛ inch (2 mm).

Turn the fabric over so that the right sides are now facing each other, and enclose the seam allowances.

Pin along the first sewing lines.

Tack, stitch and press. (2)

Turn the fabric over so that the reverse sides are facing each other. Press.

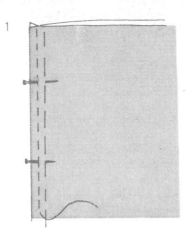

1

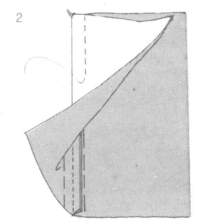

2

Finishing curved seams

On a curved seam, where you will have snipped into the seam allowance fairly frequently, you should always oversew by hand. Any other method of finishing would create too much bulk.

Finishing partly curved, partly straight seams

Snip into the material at the beginning and end of the curved part of the seam so that the material of this curved part lies flat. Finish as for curved seam.

For the straight part of the seam you can use any of the relevant techniques described in this lesson.

The couture touch

Hooks and bars

Hooks-and-eyes or bars are not very attractive additions to a dress. In couture they are usually concealed.

Cover the hook with a blanket-stitch (page 79). Work the stitches very close together. Use a double thread. Make sure the colour of your thread and that of your fabric match. (3)

3

You can, if you wish, cover the bar in the same way as the hook. Alternatively you can make an embroidered bar. To do this:

Make a loop of three double threads and then cover these at right angles with blanket-stitches. Again make sure that thread and fabric match. (4)

4

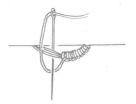

Snap fasteners

Snap fasteners which are placed so that they are visible should be covered with chiffon.

From the chiffon cut out two circles, each of them twice the diameter of the snap.

Place each half of the snap face downwards in the middle of one of the circles.

Sew a running stitch around the circumference of each circle. Work the ball, that is the protruding part, of the snap through the chiffon. Pull the threads up and sew the chiffon together. Repeat with the other half and attach the two halves of the snap to the dress. (5)

5

Rouleau

A rouleau is often used in couture as a means of finishing a neckline or sleeves. It is really a narrow bias binding. (6)

A rouleau is always cut on the bias. It is attached to the edge of the neckline in the same way as a tie-collar.

To turn out the tie-part of the rouleau use a bodkin or a small safety pin.

6

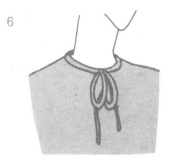

LESSON 11

Skirts

Skirt with waistband

A waistband must be given extra firmness if it is to hold your skirt in position. This can be done by lining it with a ribbon.

Make up a waistband

With the reverse side up, place the waistband on the table so that the edge with the balance marks is the one further away from you. (1)

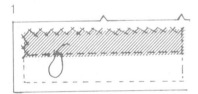

Place the ribbon on top of the waistband so that one edge lies along the sewing line furthest away from you and the other edge lies on the fold line.

Slip-stitch the ribbon to the waistband along the sewing line and the fold line.

With the right sides together, fold the waistband lengthways in half.

Stitch the two short ends together. Do not stitch the seam allowances together. Press and trim. (2)

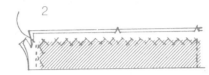

Turn out the waistband so that the reverse sides are together.

Fold under the seam allowance of the long edge with no balance marks.

Tack. Press without removing the tacking.

Attach the waistband to the skirt

With the right sides together, join the long edge of the waistband which has the balance marks to the skirt.

Match sewing lines and balance marks.

Pin, tack, stitch, press, trim and layer.

Turn the waistband over the fold line so that it encloses all the cut edges. Pin.

Slip-stitch the free edge of the waistband to the skirt. (3)

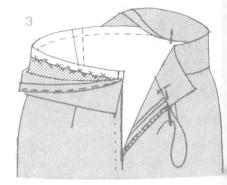

Remove the tacking and press lightly.

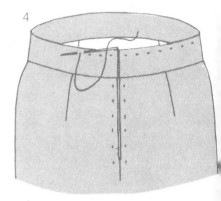

To keep the waistband from twisting, you can prick-stitch from the right side of the fabric. (4)

Guide to buying ribbons

Petersham ribbons. These are fairly stiff ribbons.

They may be straight or curved and with or without boning.

They are available in different widths and weights, but only in black or white.

Grosgrain ribbons. These are much softer and easier to shape.

You can buy them in many different colours and widths.

The choice of ribbon is a matter of personal taste, depending in the main on whether you prefer a firm or a soft finish.

To prevent the waistband from twisting and creasing, your ribbon should be exactly the same width as the finished waistband.

Skirt without waistband

All skirts need extra support at the waist. In skirts without waistbands this can be given by a firm ribbon attached to the inside of the waist seam.

Most skirt tops are curved, and you must therefore make your ribbon follow the curve of the skirt top.

You do this by pressing the ribbon with a steam iron or under a damp cloth. You ought to have no difficulty in making the ribbon the same shape as the skirt top, as under steam it will become quite pliable. Use your pattern as a guide.

Let the ribbon dry completely before attaching it.

Attach the ribbon to the skirt.

Turn the skirt to the reverse side. Place the ribbon in the seam allowance so that the shorter, or inner, curve of the ribbon lies at the sewing line. Tack. (5)

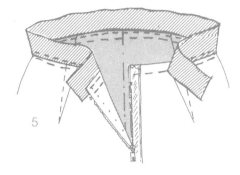

5

Stitch and then fold the ribbon to the inside of the skirt and press lightly.

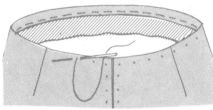

6

As the cut edge of the seam allowance will be hidden by the lining, you do not need to do any finishing.

To keep the ribbon in place

Prick-stitch the top edge of the skirt to the ribbon. Do this on the right side of the material. Sew about ⅛ inch (2 mm) below the waist seam. This will prevent the ribbon from turning inside out. (6)

All skirts should be lined. Later on in this book you will be shown how to make up the lining and attach it by hand to the skirt.

Working with different fabrics

Very light, transparent or loosely woven fabrics

To prevent the ribbon from showing through, line the waistband. For this you can use your lining fabric.

Heavy or bulky fabrics

When cutting, you can lay out the pattern of the waistband so that the edge without the balance marks lies on the selvage. This will obviate the need to turn the fabric over when attaching the free edge of the waistband to the skirt. If the selvage is too tight, snip into it at intervals and oversew by hand.

When cutting out the waistband, make its width equal the finished width of the waistband plus two seam allowances.

If you have no selvage left, you can oversew the cut edge by hand, but only if your fabric is one which does not fray badly.

LESSON 12

Hemlines

In this lesson you will be shown how to finish hemlines on straight skirts and full skirts.

Straight skirt

Mark the hemline. Allow 2½ inches (6 cm) turning for the hem. To mark the hemline you will find it easier if you ask a friend to help you.

Try on the dress. Ask your friend to measure the distance from the floor to the hemline, using a ruler rather than a tape-measure, because a ruler is firmer and more accurate.

Mark this same distance all round the hem with pins. Take off the skirt, and put a running stitch along the line indicated by the pins.

Finish the cut edge of the hem

Finish the cut edge by oversewing it by hand or overlocking it by machine, or, if the fabric is not too heavy, turning the fabric under.

Below the hemline trim the seam allowance to ¼ inch (5 mm). (1)

Join the hem to the skirt

Turn the material over at the fold line so that reverse sides face each other.

Pin, placing the pins at right angles to the fold line. Tack ¼ inch (5 mm) from the fold line. (2)

Remove the pins.

Press along the fold line without removing the tacking. (Remember to use brown paper. Take care not to over-press.)

Make sure that the seams on the hem will meet the corresponding seams on the skirt.

Pin the hem again to the skirt, placing the pins at right angles to the fold line. Tack about ½ inch (1 cm) from the edge.

Attach the edge of the hem to the garment by hand, using an invisible stitch (page 78). Do not pull your sewing thread tight. (3)

Remove tacking and press lightly.

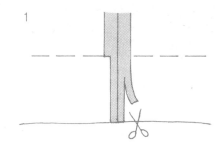

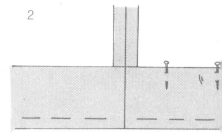

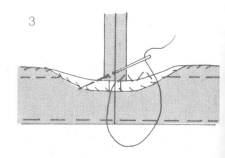

Full skirt

Allow only 1 ¼ inches (3 cm) for the hem.

For very full skirts you can reduce the width of the hem even more.

Mark the fold line, that is where you want the skirt to end, with a running stitch.

Turn the hem over at the fold line.

Tack the hem to the skirt ¼ inch (5 mm) from the fold line. If there is excess fullness on the hem, this must first be eliminated.

To do this:

Stitch a gathering line ⅛ inch (2 mm) from the cut edge.

Draw up the gathering threads so that the edge of the hem and the corresponding place on the skirt coincide. Distribute the fullness evenly. Shrink out excess fullness with the point of an iron, working from the fold line to the cut edge. Be very careful not to shrink the fabric further than the cut edge. Use brown paper. (4)

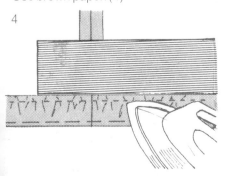

Once the hem is the same width as the corresponding part on the skirt follow the same procedure as for a straight skirt.

That is, finish the cut edge by hand and attach the hem to the skirt with an invisible stitch.

You can eliminate a small amount of excess fullness by cutting your material in a straight line at each side seam, below the hemline. You should do this only after you have established the correct length of your dress. (5)

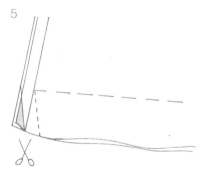

Notes:
When attaching the hem of a skirt leave some slack in your thread. If you don't the thread is likely to break when you wear the skirt.

Always press both the hem and the skirt on the straight grain.

A number of designers have recently finished the hem of jersey skirts with two rows of top-stitching.

This way of finishing a hem is quick and easy to do. The final effect can be very attractive, provided the two rows of stitching run exactly parallel with each other.

To finish hems in this way machine on the right side of the fabric. The first row of stitches should be ⅛ inch (2 mm) and the second ½ inch (7 mm) from the fold line.

To finish the hem, simply trim away all excess fabric.

LESSON 13

Necklines with facing

In these styles you will find separate pattern-pieces for facings. They match in shape and size the parts of the dress to which you attach them.

The facing must be cut on the same grain as the corresponding piece of the main material. If it is not, the two layers of material will pull and twist in opposite directions.

Round neckline

A facing is often made up of more than one pattern-piece. If it is, you must first join up all the pieces. (1)

You will find that only one edge of the completed facing has balance marks.

This is the edge which you must attach to the neckline.

Finish the edge with no balance marks, oversewing it by hand.

Pin, tack, stitch, press and then trim the seams which you have just created. (2)

With their right sides together, pin the edge of the facing which has the balance marks to the edge of the neckline.

Match at the shoulder seams and centre front and centre back.

Make sure that the two sewing lines overlap one another. Tack and stitch. (3)

Press. Use a tailor's ham. First press the seam open. Then press both seam allowances to the same side. Snip into the seam allowances to make them lie flat.

Turn the facing to the inside of the dress and tack it to the dress 1/8 inch (2 mm) below the sewing line. Tack on the right side of the dress. Press lightly on the reverse side.

1

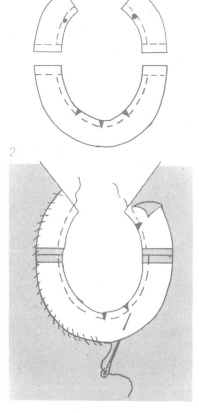

2

3

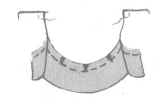

Underststitch the finished neckline

To prevent the facing from rolling to the outside you should "understitch" it.

Open out the facing and the seam allowances so that they all face in the same direction.

Sew by hand ¼ inch (5 mm) from the sewing line through all three layers, that is the facing and two seam allowances. Use small stitches.

Trim and layer the seam allowances so the seam allowance of the dress becomes the longer of the two.

Attach the facing by hand at the shoulder seams. If the dress has a centre front or centre back seam, attach it to those seams too. (4)

Press lightly.

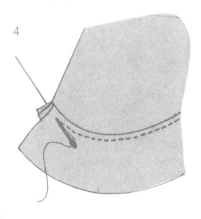

4

Round neckline with a slit at the centre

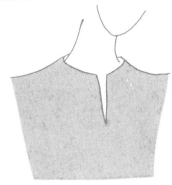

Normally you attach the interfacing of a dress to the facing. With this style you attach it directly to the reverse side of the main material. You do this to prevent ridges from showing through. (5)

For this style you should use sew-on interfacing only.

After you have attached the interfacing, attach the facing in the usual way. With the right sides together, pin the facing to the neckline of the dress. (6)

Snip into the seam allowance of the slit at the front of the neckline.

Snip as far as you can without cutting into the sewing line.

Turn the facing to the reverse side of the dress.

Tack close to the neckline, and press on the reverse side of the dress. (7)

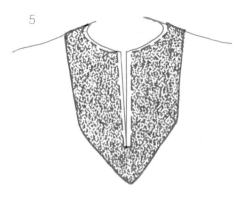

5

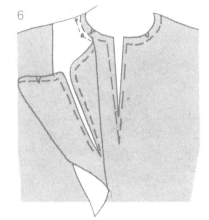

6

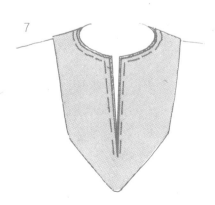

7

Square neckline

In a square neckline the corners must always be neat and strong.

To reinforce the corners of a square neckline, cut out two square patches from your lining material or from organza 1 ¼ inches (3 cm) square. If your material is a light one, such as silk, you can use this for the patches.

On the reverse side of the dress place this patch on a corner of the neckline. The centre point of the patch should lie exactly on top of the corner point of the sewing line. Pin. (1)

Tack the patch to the neckline along the sewing line.

Repeat the same procedure with the other patch at the other corner of the neckline.

Make up the facing

The front facing for square necklines should be cut in one piece and joined to the back neck facing at the shoulder seam.

Join the facing to the neckline

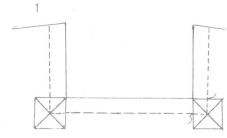

With the right sides together, pin the facing to the neckline. Match all sewing lines and balance marks. Tack. (2)

Stitch very carefully at the corners, pivoting your needle.

Press lightly from the reverse side.

Be careful not to stretch the neckline when pressing. Always hold the fabric down with one hand and pull it very gently in the direction of the lengthways grain. You must press only in the direction of the lengthways grain.

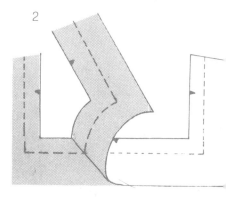

Trim the seam allowances to ¼ inch (5 mm). Trim the patches to the same size as the seam allowances.

Snip into the corner of the neckline as far as you can go without cutting into the sewing line. (3)

Turn the facing to the inside of the dress, making sure that the seam is not visible from the right side.

On the right side tack down near the sewing line. Press lightly.

Remember not to use a patch when working with transparent fabrics.

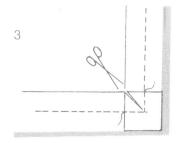

LESSON 14

Necklines with facing and front openings

For these styles the facings should be interfaced to give the front opening more support.

In many patterns the front facing is not a separate pattern-piece but a part of the front of the dress.

Interface the front facings and back neck facings on the reverse side of the fabric.

With the right sides together, join the front and back facings at the shoulder line. (4)

Turn the facings to the right side. With the right sides together, attach the facing to the neckline of the dress.

Pin, tack, stitch, press, trim and layer.

Snip into the seam allowance to make the fabric lie flat. Snip diagonally across at the corners. (5)

Turn the facing to the inside of the dress.

From the right side tack the facing to the dress close to the neckline and to the front edge. Press.

Attach the facing by hand to the seam allowances at the shoulder.

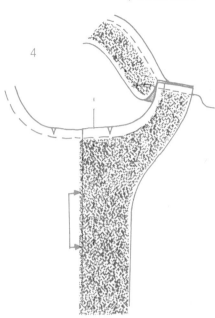

4

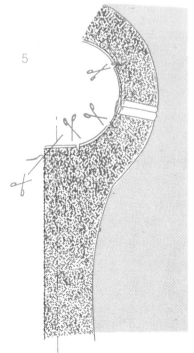

5

LESSON 15

Necklines with stand-up collars

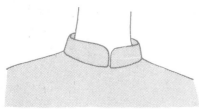

There are many different styles of collar from which you can choose. But if you look closely you will see that every one of them is based on the same principle as the bias binding. Like the bias binding, the collar encloses the cut edges of the neckline—between two layers of fabric.

The simplest type of collar, and the one which most closely resembles a bias binding, is the stand-up collar.

Make up a stand-up collar

A collar will keep its shape better if it is interfaced. You can interface one or both layers of the collar according to the degree of firmness you want.

With the right sides together fold the collar lengthways in half.

Pin together the two short ends. Tack and stitch only from the fold line to the sewing line.

Press. First set the stitches.

Then press open the seams. This creates a neat edge on the right side of the collar.

Trim to ⅛ inch (2 mm) at the seams. At the corner cut across as near to the sewing line as you dare, without cutting into the stitching. Turn the collar out so that the two reverse sides are together. (1)

Fold the seam allowance which has no balance marks under at the sewing line. Press without removing the tacking.

Attach the collar to the neckline of a dress

A collar is attached in exactly the same way as a bias binding.

With the right sides together, pin the edge of the collar which has the balance marks to the neckline of the dress.

Match the sewing lines and the balance marks. (2)

Tack, stitch, press, trim.

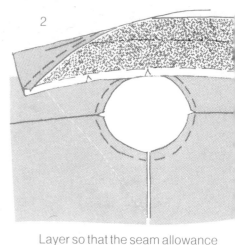

2

Layer so that the seam allowance of the dress becomes the shorter.

Complete the collar

Fold the collar over so that all the cut edges are enclosed.

Attach the free edge to the neckline, by hand. Use a slip-stitch. (3)

Collars come in a variety of styles. The techniques described in this lesson will enable you to make up any of these.

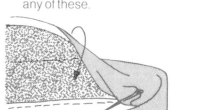

3

LESSON 16

Necklines with tie-collars

First complete the front of the blouse.

With the right sides together stitch the facing to the neckline between •...• Press and trim. Turn the blouse to the right side ready for putting on the collar.

Make up a tie-collar

When you come to making up the tie-collar, interface the collar part but not the tie. (Interfacing would make the tie too bulky.)

With the right sides facing each other, fold the tie-collar lengthways in two. Pin together the two short ends and the parts of the long edges belonging to the tie. (4)

Tack, stitch, press.

Trim as for enclosed seams.

Snip into the seam allowances of both layers of fabric as shown on the diagram. (5)

Turn out the tie-collar so that the reverse sides are now facing each other.

Fold the edge which has no balance marks under. Tack and press lightly.

Attach the tie-collar to the neckline

When you attach a tie-collar to a neckline you must leave a space of about 1¼ inches (3 cm) on either side of the centre front. This will leave you room to knot the tie.

Pin the edge of the collar-part with balance marks to the edge of the neckline. Match balance marks and sewing lines. (6)

Tack, stitch, trim and layer.

Turn over the collar-part so that all seam allowances are enclosed. Attach the free edge to the neckline by hand. (7)

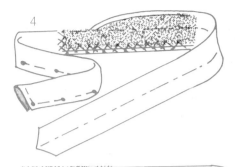

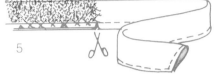

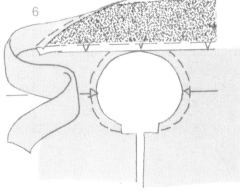

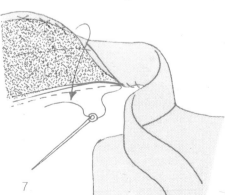

LESSON 17

Necklines with facing and collar combined

As you can see from the illustration this collar is made up of two parts:

The lower part which forms the lapel.

The upper part which is the collar proper.

Make up the lapel

Interface the facings. You learnt how to do this in earlier lessons.

With the right sides together, pin the interfaced facing to that part of the neckline which will not be covered by the collar. Your pattern will indicate this clearly. (1)

Tack, stitch.

Press in the direction of the lengthways grain.

Trim as for enclosed seams.

Snip diagonally into the seam allowance at the end of your stitching.

Turn the facing to the inside of the dress.

Tack the facing to the unfinished part of the neckline along the sewing line.

By hand attach the shoulder end of the facing to the dress at the shoulder seams. (2)

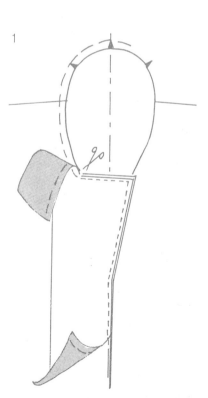

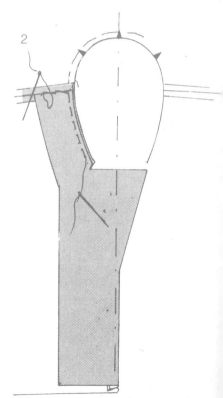

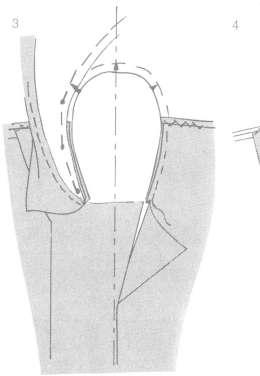

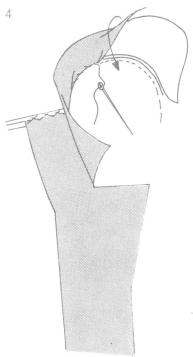

Make up the collar

Interface and make up your collar in exactly the same way as you learnt in the previous lesson.

Attach the collar to the neckline

Join the edge of the collar which has the balance marks to the cut edge of the neckline. The right side of the collar should face the reverse side of the neckline.

Make sure that the sewing line of one is exactly on top of the sewing line of the other. Match all balance marks. (3)

Between the front end of the collar and the shoulder seam there are three layers of fabric through which you must pin. These are the bodice, the facing and the collar. At the back of the collar, between the shoulder seams, there are only two layers, that is the bodice and the collar.

Pin, tack, stitch, press, trim and layer. Remove all tacking.

Turn the collar over so that all seam allowances are enclosed.

Slip-stitch the free edge of the collar to the neckline. (4)

Notes:
There are a number of ways in which you can attach a collar. The method described in this lesson obviates the need for a facing at the back of the neck.

It is probably the easiest technique to learn and also one which is commonly used in couture.

Make sure that when you attach the collar to the neckline, you stitch the edge which will be visible, that is the one next to your neck, and finish by hand the one which will not be visible.

The success of making a shirt collar depends on the accuracy with which you work. You must match all balance marks and sewing lines exactly.

There are many attractive variations on this style of collar. The techniques for making and attaching them are the same, though the collars vary in appearance because of their cut.

The shallower the curve of the collar the flatter the collar will lie. A stand-away effect is achieved by increasing the curve of the collar.

LESSON 18

Set-in sleeves

You may well find it much easier than you expected to make up and set in a sleeve.

You will not be required to learn any new techniques. Those you will be using have already been explained.

There are a number of different styles of sleeves. The main types, described here, are:

Set-in

Raglan

Kimono

Dolman

Set-in sleeve with a hem

Prepare the sleeve

Stitch two rows of gathering lines on the upper edge (sometimes called the cap) of the sleeve as indicated in your pattern. (1)

Join up the under-arm sleeve. (Pin, tack, stitch, press, trim.)

Finish the hem of the sleeve

Follow the same procedure as for the hem of a skirt. This is set out in full on page 98 and can be summarized as follows:

Mark the fold line, that is the finished length of the sleeve.

Turn the sleeve to the reverse side.

Finish the cut edge of the sleeve.

Turn over the hem at the fold line.

Pin, tack and press. (Use a sleeve-board.)

Attach the finished edge of the hem to the sleeve by hand. Use an invisible stitch (page 78). (2)

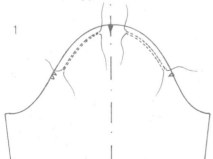

1

2

Press lightly.

Turn the sleeve back to the right side.

Set in the sleeve

Turn the dress to the reverse side. With the right sides together place the sleeve into the armhole. Make sure that the front of the sleeve meets the front of the armhole. Similarly the back of the sleeve must meet the back of the armhole.

Pin together at the under-arm seam and at all balance marks. The top of the sleeve must always meet the end of the shoulder seam.

Place the pins diagonally to the sewing line. Work from the sleeve side. (3)

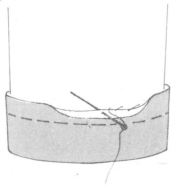

3

On one side of the sleeve pull up both gathering threads between < •===• > so that on that side the circumference of the sleeve and that of the armhole become the same.

Secure the gathering threads by winding them at both ends around a pin in a figure of 8.

With the tip of a pin distribute fullness evenly between balance marks and secure with more pins.

Repeat the procedure on the other half of the sleeve. (4)

Tack the sleeve into place.

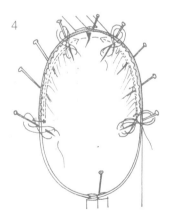

Try on the garment

Even if you work with a perfectly adjusted pattern, it is advisable to try on the garment when the sleeves are only tacked in. Even a small error made when cutting the fabric can unbalance the hang of the sleeve.

Excess fullness

As you can see the circumference of the sleeve is greater than that of

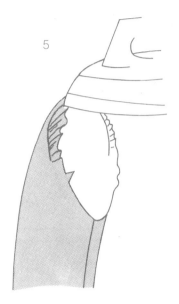

the armhole. This is to give the extra fullness needed to accommodate the curve of your upper arm.

Unfortunately it may also create unattractive gathers and creases at the sewing line where extra fullness is not needed.

In a pattern which has been adjusted to your own measurements this excess fullness will be relatively slight and easy to shrink out. You do this as follows:

Remove the sleeve from the armhole, being careful not to alter the distribution of the gathers.

Place the sleeve over a tailor's ham. Shrink with a damp cloth. Apply only the tip of the iron, and shrink only from the edge of the seam allowance to the sewing line. If you were to go any further you would shrink away essential fullness. Hold the iron fractionally above the fabric so that steam can circulate freely. (5)

To check whether you have really eliminated all excess fullness, hold up the sleeve. Then, from the right side, turn the seam allowance over at the sewing line. Your sleeve should be perfectly smooth along the sewing line, with no gathers showing. (6)

If your fabric is wholly shrink-resistant, try to ease out the excess fullness by working with your fingertips, that is distribute the excess fullness between the balance marks so evenly that when you turn over the seam allowance virtually no gathers are visible. When you are satisfied with the result, set in your sleeve.

With the right sides together, place the sleeve back into the armhole. Pin at the under-arm seams, the centre top and all other markings. Place pins at right angles to the sewing line. Make sure that one sewing line is exactly on top of the other.

Tack.

Stitch on the reverse side of the sleeve. Guide the fabric to make sure no gathers form. (1)

Stitch a second row as a guard-line ⅛ inch (2 mm) in the seam allowance.

Trim to the guard-line and oversew by hand. (2)

If you have already pre-shrunk your material or prepared it in other ways for washing, you may wonder whether it is possible to shrink it further, as required in this lesson.

In many cases, this will be possible provided you apply the shrinking process to the right areas.

All fabrics stretch and shrink more on the bias than on the straight or cross-grain. The part of the sleeve which you shrink is on the bias.

This is the reason why you don't gather across the top of the sleeve.

LESSON 19

Raglan, kimono and dolman sleeves

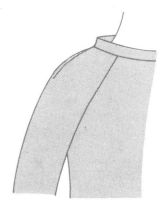

1

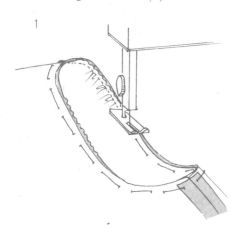

2

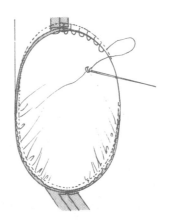

Raglan sleeve

In a raglan sleeve the additional fullness needed is created by a curved seam or by a dart at the shoulder seam. Alternatively, you can create fullness by gathering, beginning at the neckline.

As you learnt about curved seams, darts and gathering in earlier lessons, you ought to have no difficulty with a raglan sleeve.

First complete the sleeve. Then join the under-arm seam.

To set the sleeve in: with the right sides together pin the sleeve into the armhole. (3)

Match at the under-arm seam and at all balance marks. Tack.

Stitch from the reverse side of the sleeve.

Stitch a guard-line between the markings shown on your pattern.

Clip the seam allowance at the two ends of the guard-line.

Trim very close to the guard-line. Oversew by hand. (4)

Press the seams open above the guard-line.

To finish a raglan sleeve you can either hem it or add a cuff in the same way as for a set-in sleeve.

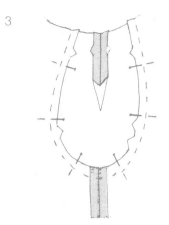

3

4

Kimono sleeve

A kimono sleeve is cut with the bodice in one piece.

Considerable strain is exerted on the curved part of the under-arm seam. You should therefore reinforce the curved part of the sleeve with a narrow tape, $\frac{1}{4}$ inch (5 mm) wide. The tape should measure about 1 $\frac{1}{2}$ inches (4 cm) each side of the centre of the curve. (5)

After that treat the under-arm seam as you would any curved seam, and snip into the seam allowances to make them lie flat.

Dolman sleeve

A dolman sleeve is similar to a kimono sleeve, but much wider and cut lower. As there is far less strain on this type of sleeve there is no need to put in a tape. (6)

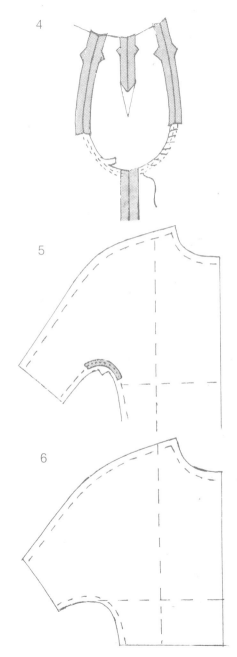

5

6

LESSON 20

Sleeves with cuffs

The cuff of a sleeve is usually made narrow enough to fit a wrist. To be able to put your hand through a cuff, therefore, you must be able to open it up.

There are a number of ways in which you can do this. Most of them use techniques which you have already learnt, but when applied to a sleeve they can be excessively time-consuming and, because you have to work with a comparatively small area, are difficult to carry out to perfection.

In this lesson you will be shown one method which is simple, produces an attractive result, and is frequently used in couture.

This method may or may not be the one which is shown in your pattern. If it is not, you can still use it.

Prepare the sleeve

Stitch two rows of gathering lines round the top of the sleeve between markings, as indicated in your pattern. (1)

Stitch two rows of gathering lines along the bottom edge of the sleeve, again as indicated in your pattern. (1)

On the bottom edge of the pattern you will see two identical markings.

Snip into the seam allowance at both these markings as far as the sewing line. (2)

Trim the seam allowance between the two markings to ½ inch (1 cm).

Turn the sleeve to the reverse side.

Oversew the cut edges of the seam allowance between ▼.....▼ by hand. (3)

Turn this part of the seam allowance over at the fold line and slip-stitch it to the reverse side of the sleeve. Press lightly.

Join the under-arm seam. (Pin, tack, stitch, trim.)

1

2
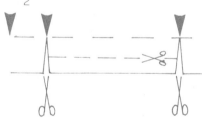

3
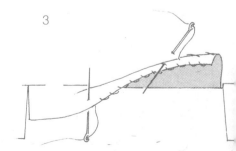

Prepare the cuff

A cuff may be said to resemble the waistband of a skirt. You make both in much the same way as you make a bias binding.

Interface the cuff as on page 96. You can interface all or only half the cuff.

With the right sides together fold the cuff in half.

Stitch the two short ends and part of the long edge together as indicated in the pattern. Snip into both layers of the seam allowance. Press and trim, following the rules for enclosed seams. (4)

Fold over the seam allowance of the edge which has no balance marks.

Tack.

Press without removing the tacking.

Turn the cuff to the right side.

Join the cuff to the sleeve

With the right sides together pin the edge of the cuff which has the balance marks to the edge of the sleeve.

Match balance marks and sewing lines.

Draw up the gathering threads on the bottom edge of the sleeve until the sleeve and the cuff are the same length.

Distribute the gathering evenly between the balance marks.

Pin, tack, stitch, trim and layer.

Turn the sleeve to the reverse side.

Turn the cuff over at the fold line so that all seam allowances are enclosed, and attach the free edge of the cuff to the sleeve by hand. (5)

To set in the sleeve, follow the instructions on page 108.

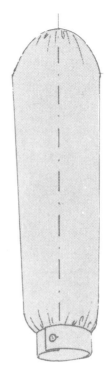

Working with different fabrics

If you have chosen very light or transparent fabric, line your cuffs before interfacing them.

Use sew-on interfacing only.

5

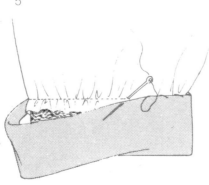

4

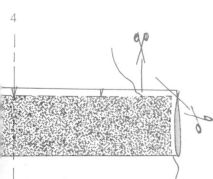

Zips

In this lesson you will learn about the different types of zip which you can buy and how to sew them into garments.

All zips must be sewn in by hand.

There are a number of types of zip on the market. They vary in weight and length and in the materials from which they are made.

There are several ways of inserting a zip in a garment. Here you will be taught only one of them. This is a method frequently used in couture.

It is easy to learn and suitable for most garments. (Not, please note, for trousers, with which this book does not deal.)

Zips are normally sewn into a seam, such as the centre back seam or a side seam.

Preparation

Tack down the seam allowances in the opening left for the zip. Press.

Sew in your zip

Place your garment right side up on the table. Place the closed zip in the seam opening.

The tab should be ¼ inch (5 mm) below the sewing line. The bottom stop of the zip should be ½ inch (1 cm) below the seam opening.

Pin the zip into place.

Pin from the top down on both sides of the zip, then across at the bottom. (1)

The seam opening should meet along the centre of the zip.

Open the zip and tack it into place.

Tack from the top down on both sides of the zip, then across at the bottom.

Sew the zip in by hand, using prick-stitching (see page 79).

Sew from the top down on both sides of the zip, then across at the bottom. (2)

Remove all tacking.

Press lightly, avoiding the teeth of the zip. (You can press round the edges of the zip on the right side of the material provided you use a dry ironing-cloth.)

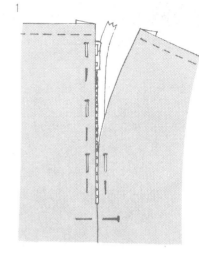

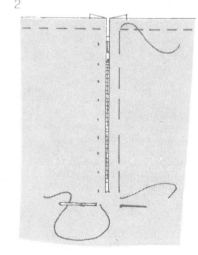

Zip at the neckline

Attach the facing to the neckline first.

The tab of the zip should be ¼ inch (5 mm) below the sewing line. Then set in your zip, as explained opposite.

Open up the facing. Tack the top of the zip to the sewing line. Press lightly.

Fold the facing over so that it encloses the top of the zip. If necessary, trim the short ends of the facing diagonally to clear the teeth of the zip. (3)

Finish at the neckline with a hook and bar.

Skirt without a waistband

Use the same method as above.

Skirt with a waistband

Set the zip into the seam of the skirt.

The tab of the zip should be ¼ inch (5 mm) below the sewing line.

Join the waistband to the skirt. (4)

Trim the tape of the zip to the sewing line of the waistband.

Turn the waistband over so that it encloses the top of the zip.

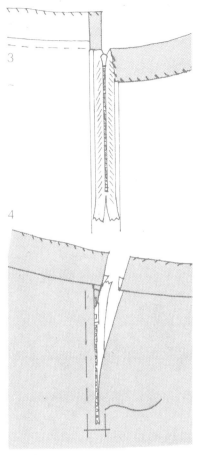

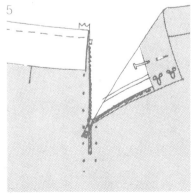

Attach the free edge of the waistband to the reverse side of the skirt.

Finish the two short edges of the waistband by hand. Sew on hooks and eyes. (5)

Guide to buying zips

Heavyweight zips. These have cotton tape and metal teeth and are suitable for trousers, coats, anoraks and other garments made of heavy fabrics.

Lightweight zips. These have man-made fibre tape and teeth and are suitable for most dress fabrics.

Colour. Zips are manufactured in a wide variety of colours, and you should have no difficulty in finding a colour to match your garment.

Invisible zips. There are a number of so-called invisible zips on the market. They are not suitable for the methods described in this chapter.

Working with different fabrics

Stretch fabrics. Stretch the fabric *slightly* when you are pinning it on to the zip.

Chiffon. Don't use a zip for chiffon garments. Use small buttons and loops instead.

LESSON 22

Pockets

In this lesson you will learn how to make:

Round patch pockets

Square patch pockets

Pockets in side seams

Round patch pocket

With the right sides together join the top edge of the pocket to the top edge of the lining. (1)

Stitch a gathering line along the curved parts of both the pocket and the lining. (2)

Pull up the gathering threads around the curved parts.

Cut away excess fullness as shown in the illustration. Trim. (3)

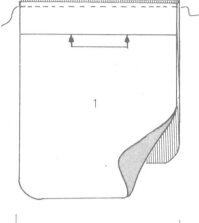

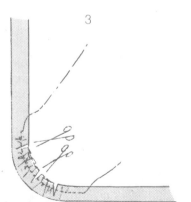

Fold the pocket along the fold line so that the reverse sides face each other.

Slip-stitch the lining to the pocket, making sure that the lining does not come quite to the edge of the pocket. (4)

Tack and press from the lining side.

Place the pocket on the garment. Pin, tack and slip-stitch. (5)

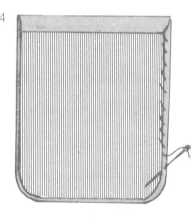

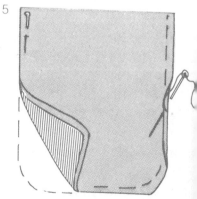

Square patch pocket

When making up a square pocket you should, in general, follow the instructions given for a rounded pocket.

The only difference is that, in order to eliminate excess fullness at the corners, instead of gathering you use a technique called mitring.

To make up your pocket

With the right sides together, join your lining to the main fabric at the sewing lines.

Lay out your fabric, with the reverse side up, on your table. (6)

Fold all the seam allowances towards the inside. Press. (7)

Open up the seam allowances.

Fold diagonally across each corner so that the diagonal fold line coincides with the corner of the sewing line. Press.

Trim the corner to ½ inch (1 cm) from the diagonal fold line. (8)

Without disturbing the diagonal fold turn the seam allowances back towards the centre. (9)

Slip-stitch the mitred edges together. (10)

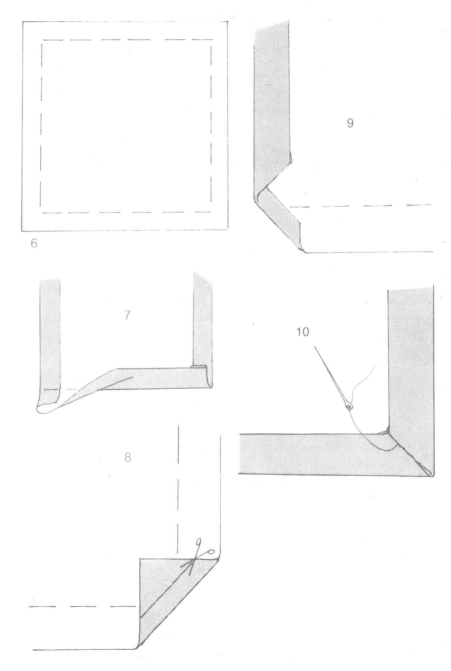

Pockets in side seams

Place the front of the garment on the table with the right side up.

With the right sides together join the pocket to the skirt. Join at the "stitching line for pocket" indicated on the pattern. Make sure that the fuller part of the pocket is the one nearer the hem. (1)

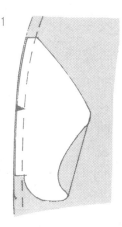

Press.

Repeat the same process for the back of the skirt.

With the right sides facing each other pin and tack the side seams together, leaving open the part of the seam where the pocket comes. (2)

Pin together the two layers of the pocket.

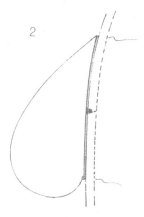

Start stitching from the top down. When you reach the pocket, pivot and stitch the outer edge of the pocket.

Pivot and carry on stitching the part of the side seam which lies below the pocket. Press. (3)

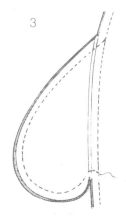

Turn the pocket along the fold line towards the front of the skirt.

Press the side seams open.

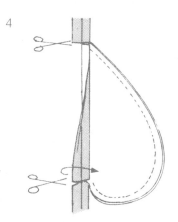

Snip into the back seam allowance as shown in the illustration. This will allow the seam to lie open above and below the pocket. (4)

Press.

LESSON 23

Lining

Why do you need lining?

Lining improves the appearance of a dress. It also makes it more comfortable to wear.

When a dress has been lined the main material is given support, the dress hangs better and does not cling, and the finish on the inside is neater.

There are two forms of lining:

Loose lining

Mounting

Loose lining

For this you make up your dress and your lining separately and then join them together.

Cut out your lining

The patterns for some dresses include special pattern-pieces for the lining. In other cases you use the same pattern-pieces as for the dress.

Make up your lining

Make up your lining in the same way as you made up your dress.

When you have finished your lining, hang it up, ready for use.

Attach the lining to the dress

If you have a dressmaker's dummy, put the dress, with the reverse side out, on it.

Alternatively, place your dress on a hanger in a position which allows you to move around it.

Slip the lining over the dress with the two reverse sides together.

Pin the lining to the dress. Start at the top and work downwards.

Slip-stitch the lining to the dress at the following points:

For a one-piece dress

Neckline
Shoulder seam
Armholes
Zip
Waist seam

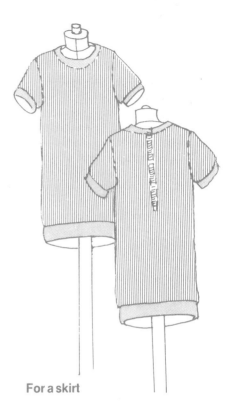

For a skirt

At the waist seam and zip

Hemlines. The lining should not be attached to the main material at the hemline. It should be hemmed and finished independently. The finished length of the lining should be ¾ inch (2 cm) shorter than the skirt in the main material.

Side seams. Do not attach the lining at the side seams. This might cause it to pull after the first cleaning.

Sleeves are not often lined, but you can line them if you wish.

Mounting

When mounting you should treat the lining material and the main fabric as one.

Lay out your lining fabric. Place the pieces of your pattern on your fabric.

Mark the sewing lines, balance marks and any other symbols. Cut out the pieces of lining.

Lay out your main fabric in a single layer, with the reverse side up.

With the right side up, lay out the pieces of lining on your material exactly as you would lay out the pieces of a pattern.

The difference is that, unlike pattern-pieces, the pieces of lining have seam allowances on them.

Secure the pieces of the lining to the main fabric with pins and weights.

There is no need to mark the cutting line on the main fabric.

Cut out the main fabric along the cutting lines of the lining.

Stay-stitch the two layers of fabric together at the sewing lines, at all balance marks and at the centre lines.

From here on treat them as if they were one fabric.

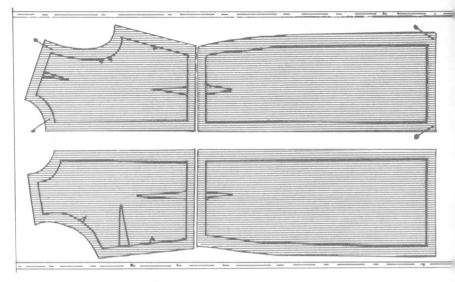

There is no hard and fast rule telling you when you should choose loose lining and when you should mount a dress.

Loose lining is easier to deal with.

In mounting a number of problems may arise because you are working with two layers of material. And when you think you have finished the dress you will still have to finish the inside.

It may be wisest to loose-line, except in the following cases:

Very loosely woven fabrics.

Fabrics which are difficult to mark. (When mounting you will be marking only the lining material.)

Translucent materials, such as white flannel or other fabrics in which the seam allowances show through to the right side of the dress. With such materials you have really no choice.

Remember this when choosing your material. For translucent materials use a fine lawn for mounting, and finish the dress with a loose lining.

To finish the inside of a dress, which you have mounted, oversew the cut edges by hand.

Alternatively, you can attach a loose lining.

In this case use a very light fabric (such as lawn) for mounting.

Your lining material should not fray badly, but if it does, oversew the seam allowances of the finished lining by hand.

How to choose lining material

These are materials which are specially manufactured to be used as lining.

You can, if you prefer, make your lining from a material not primarily designed for that purpose. In making your choice remember that your lining material must complement your main material and not change its look or feel.

For soft, light fabrics

If your main material is soft or light, the lining should enhance these qualities. As a test, place a piece of the lining material you are thinking of buying under the main material, and move the two together. Study the effect. Normally, your lining should be lighter in weight than the main material.

Your dress and its lining will be cleaned together. So the materials must react in the same way to the process chosen, whether it is washing or dry-cleaning. In other words, if you intend to wash your dress, choose a washable lining.

For very light and transparent fabrics

If your main material is a very light or transparent one; such as chiffon or organza, you will have difficulty in finding a lining material which does not change the essential character of the main material. For such fabrics make a slip as an alternative to loose lining.

This will allow the material to hang freely and retain all its original character. The finished garment will also look better. When choosing a material for the slip you should be guided by the same considerations as in the choice of lining.

Colour of lining

If your main material is not transparent, your choice of colour for your lining can be fairly wide. In general you are likely to get the best effect by having the lining in the same colour as the main material or slightly lighter.

Transparent materials, on the other hand, can easily be ruined by a lining or a slip of the wrong colour.

Place a piece of the main material on your naked arm. Place some of the proposed lining under half the material. Ideally there should be no difference in the colour of the main material when it is against your skin and when it is on the lining. At the most a very small difference in colour is permissible.

Do not assume that a flesh-coloured lining will necessarily be suitable. You may well be surprised when you see which colours do in fact give the right effect.

Black and white materials are in a category of their own. For them you can only use a black or white lining or slip.

Before buying a transparent fabric, make sure that you can find the right colour lining. Transparent fabrics, especially printed ones, can look very disappointing against the wrong lining.

Guide to lining materials

Main material	Possible linings
Cotton	Lawn
Silk	Silk
Wool	Silk or man-made fabric
Man-made	Man-made fabric
Stretch fabrics	You should never line a stretch fabric. Wear a slip instead.
Chiffon	You should never line chiffon. Instead you can wear a slip.

Man-made lining fabrics include a material which closely resembles silk. It is light and pliable, comes in many colours and is suitable for most fabrics.

Buttonholes

Buttonholes can be made by hand or by machine. Which method you choose is partly a question of taste, but you have also to consider whether your machine is one of those which can make buttonholes up to professional standard. Couture clothes normally have buttonholes made by hand, but with certain materials, particularly cotton and cotton jersey, machine-made buttonholes can be perfectly satisfactory.

Machine-made buttonholes are made after the interfacing and the facing have been attached to the part of the dress where the buttonholes go. To make the buttonholes, you stitch through all layers, that is main fabric, interfacing and facing.

By contrast, when you make buttonholes by hand, you work with only one layer of fabric. In other words, you complete your buttonhole before the interfacing and the facing are attached.

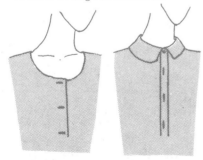

Vertical or horizontal buttonholes

Buttonholes can be vertical or horizontal. Horizontal buttonholes tend to be stronger and are commonly found in dresses. Vertical buttonholes are used mainly in narrow strips of material, such as the placket of a tailored shirt.

Your paper pattern always shows clearly where buttons and buttonholes are to be placed.

Size of buttonhole

The average width, that is shorter side of a buttonhole, is ¼ inch (6 mm). Each lip is normally ⅛ inch (3 mm) wide. These dimensions can be increased for bulky fabrics and decreased for very light ones.

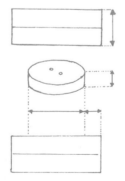

The length of a buttonhole depends on the size of the button. As a general guide, the length should be the diameter of the button and the thickness of the button plus ⅛ inch (3 mm).

Mark the size of the buttonhole on the reverse side of the fabric. Stay-stitch so that all markings are visible on both sides of the fabric.

Machine-made buttonholes

If you decide in favour of machine-made buttonholes, follow the instructions which come with the machine.

Hand-made buttonholes

For hand-made buttonholes you are recommended to adopt a method which has a rather attractive name. This is the "organza patch". It produces the most accurate results and can be used for most materials.

Working with different fabrics

For bulky fabrics or fabrics which fray easily, you should use a contrasting fabric for the lips of the buttonhole. Materials to which this applies are heavy tweed, loosely woven fabrics, velvet, embroidered fabrics and lace. Ideal substitute fabrics for the lips may be satin or dull silk. Your final choice must depend on the style of the dress.

Make sure that the colours of both fabrics match exactly both by day and in artificial light.

The "organza patch" buttonhole

Cut out a patch of organza which is ½ inch (1.5 cm) bigger on all sides than the buttonhole.

On the right side of the fabric place the organza over the buttonhole markings. (1)

Secure with pins. You will find that the sewing lines are visible through the organza. Tack the organza to the dress along the sewing lines. Start stitching at the centre of one of the long sides of the buttonholes and overlap the stitches at the end. (2)

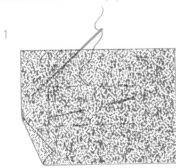

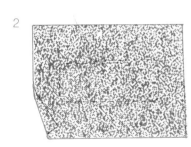

Use small stitches and pivot at the corners.

Using sharp scissors or a seam-opener, make a small opening through both layers of fabric at the centre of the buttonhole. Starting at this opening, cut diagonally to each corner, going through both layers of fabric. To avoid cutting too far in, place a pin along each short end of the buttonhole. (3)

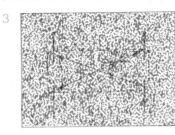

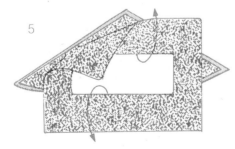

Pull the organza through the opening to the reverse side of the fabric. (4)

On the reverse side of the buttonhole press all seam allowances away from the opening. (5)

Buttonhole lips

To make the lips of a buttonhole, cut out two strips from your main fabric. Each of these should be ¾ inch (2 cm) bigger on all sides than the buttonhole.

Fold each of the strips in half lengthways. Press.

Place the strips so that the folds which you have just made meet. Tack together at the fold line, making sure that neither strip overlaps the other. (6)

Open up the strips and place them one on top of the other.

These strips now become the lips of the buttonhole. To attach them to the buttonhole:

Place the fabric which has the buttonhole right side up.

Slip the strips of fabric on the reverse side of the buttonhole so that they form two lips.

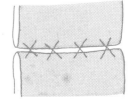

Turn the top layer of the fabric, that is the main material, towards you. You will now see five layers of seam fabric. Three are larger ones, one from organza and two from the main fabric. The other two are smaller, one being from organza and one from the main fabric. You will also see a stitching line holding the first three layers together. (1)

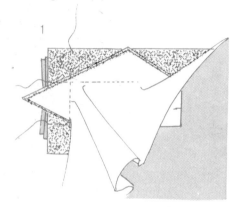

Pin all five layers together along the same stitching line.

Stitch.

Extend your stitching line about ½ inch (1 cm) at each end, machining only on the large organza and the lips.

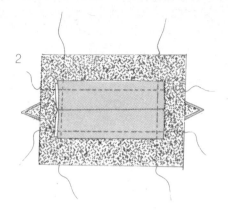

Follow the same procedure for the second long edge and then for the two shorter edges. Press.

Trim the seam allowances to about ½ inch (1 cm) and layer. (2)

Attach the facing

The technique explained here is applicable to any buttonhole on any garment, but let us suppose that the one you have made was on the front of a blouse.

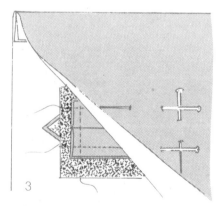

On the reverse side pin the facing to the blouse near the buttonhole. Mark the outline of the buttonhole on the facing, using pins. (3)

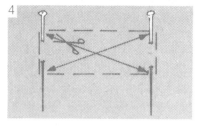

Separate the facing from the main fabric.

Using a seam-opener or scissors, slash the facing diagonally across from edge to edge. Remember to use pins at the short ends. Pin the facing back into position. Turn the cut edges under and attach the facing to the buttonhole by hand at the sewing lines. (4) (5)

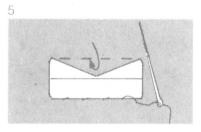

Press lightly.

It is most unlikely that the first buttonhole you make will look perfect. But after you have practised two or three times you ought not to find the work difficult.

Do not make buttonholes in a double layer of fabric, such as a hem. Remember to press at every stage in the making of buttonholes. The result will not be satisfactory unless you do.

PART THREE

EQUIPMENT

Here's advice on buying equipment and also a section on minipatterns.

Trace these patterns and make them up in calico. If you use them to follow the instructions in Part One you will learn all the tricks of the trade in the most practical way.

New aids for dressmakers are continually coming on to the market, and it is impossible in any book to provide a full list of equipment that will remain up to date for any length of time. In sewing machines in particular, new developments follow one another in rapid succession.

You will therefore be well advised to look around and see what is available, an exercise you may find both rewarding and enjoyable. The list below is confined to the most commonly used equipment and aids to dressmaking, all of which you will need sooner or later.

Bodkin. Used for drawing elastic or ribbons through casings.

Brown paper. Used in strips when pressing.

Cutting-board. One of the most important dressmaker's aids. It is made of pressed paper so that pins can be pushed into it. It can be placed over a polished table top without risk of damaging the table. A cutting-board provides an easy surface to work on and folds easily for storage. The surface

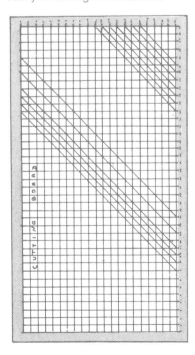

area is marked out in inches and centimetres.

Electric iron. There is a wide variety of choice. Consult manufacturers' leaflets.

Ironing-board. If you decide to buy a new board, get one which has a drying-rail and a shelf underneath.

Ironing-cloth. You can, if you wish, make this up yourself from white (not unbleached) calico.

Needle-threader.

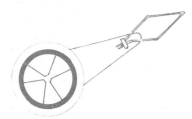

Pin-cushion.

Rulers. You should have one long and one short ruler, preferably in plastic and transparent. Curved plastic rulers are also available and are very useful for drawing or transferring curved lines.

Scissors. Different types are made for different tasks. You should have a large pair for cutting and a small pair for dressmaking. Make sure they are comfortable to use. Always keep scissors sharp, and don't use them for other purposes, such as cutting paper, which is likely to blunt them. Don't be afraid of electric scissors, which are really quite easy to use.

Seam-opener. Using one of these is the easiest way to open up a seam.

Sewing machine. Choosing a sewing machine is one of the most important decisions the home dressmaker has to face. Consult manufacturers' leaflets and ask the advice of your friends.

Sleeve-board. For pressing sleeves.

Tailor's chalk (or chalk pencils). Bought in packets. Make sure you keep the edge sharp.

Tailor's ham. For pressing curved surfaces.

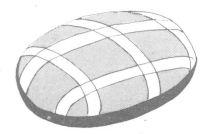

Tape-measure. One which shows imperial and metric measurements is useful.

Thimble. You really do need a good one. Make sure it is comfortable to wear.

Tissue paper (white). Used when stitching slippery fabrics, and also to protect fabrics from dirt.

Minipatterns

Minipatterns are a new aid to dressmaking.

With their help you can put into practice everything you are taught in the dressmaking lessons.This will give you the experience, and so the confidence, you need before you get down to the real business of dressmaking.

It will also be fun, because what in fact you will be doing is making miniature garments.

Don't cut the minipatterns out of the book. You may want to use them again in years to come when you have a dressmaking problem.

Instead, copy the minipatterns with the use of tracing paper. You can then use them as ordinary patterns and cut them out in mediumweight calico; remember to make the number of cut-out indicated on each minipattern. Use these cut-outs to follow the lessons.

On pages 138 to 141 you are told which cut-outs to use for the different dressmaking lessons, and also which minipatterns are necessary for interfacing, etc.

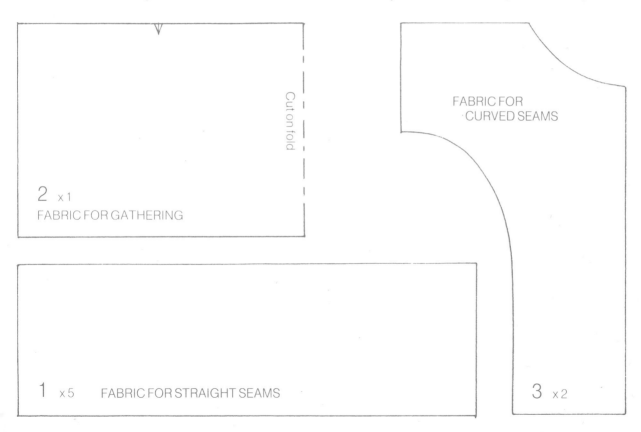

Cut on fold

2 x1
FABRIC FOR GATHERING

FABRIC FOR
CURVED SEAMS

1 x5   FABRIC FOR STRAIGHT SEAMS

3 x2

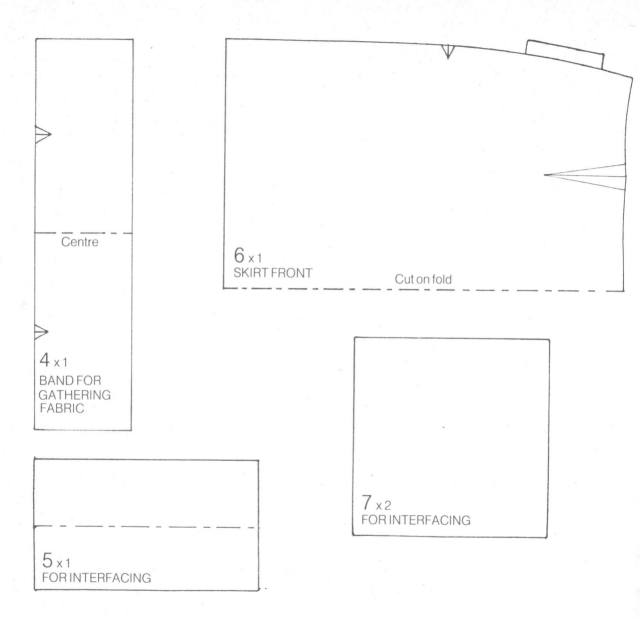

Centre

4 x 1
BAND FOR
GATHERING
FABRIC.

6 x 1
SKIRT FRONT
Cut on fold

5 x 1
FOR INTERFACING

7 x 2
FOR INTERFACING

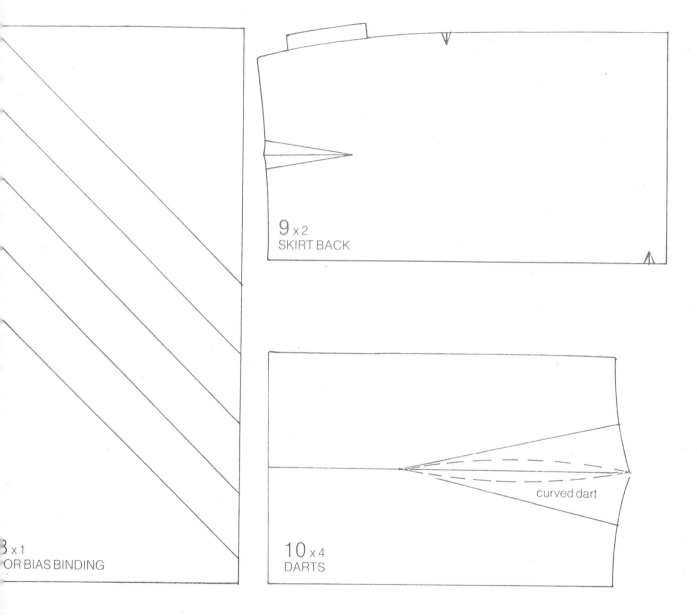

9 x2
SKIRT BACK

curved dart

10 x4
DARTS

3 x1
OR BIAS BINDING

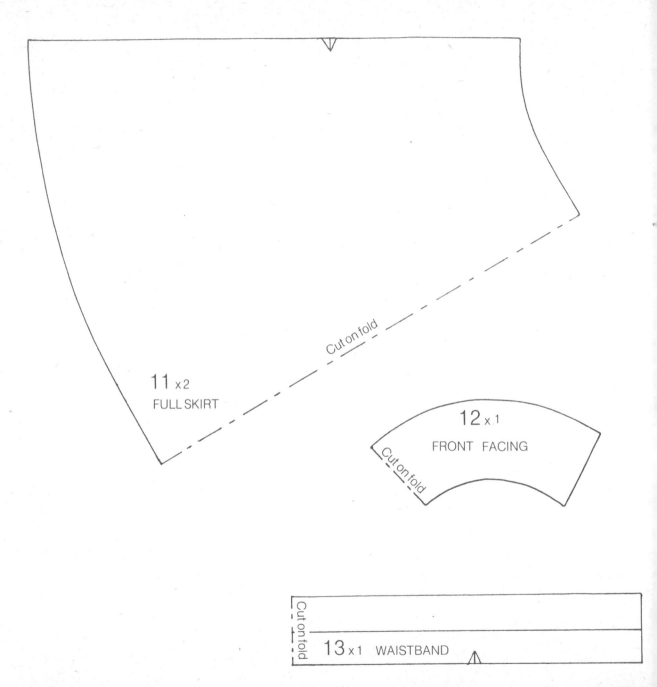

11 x2
FULL SKIRT

Cut on fold

12 x1
FRONT FACING

Cut on fold

Cut on fold
13 x1 WAISTBAND

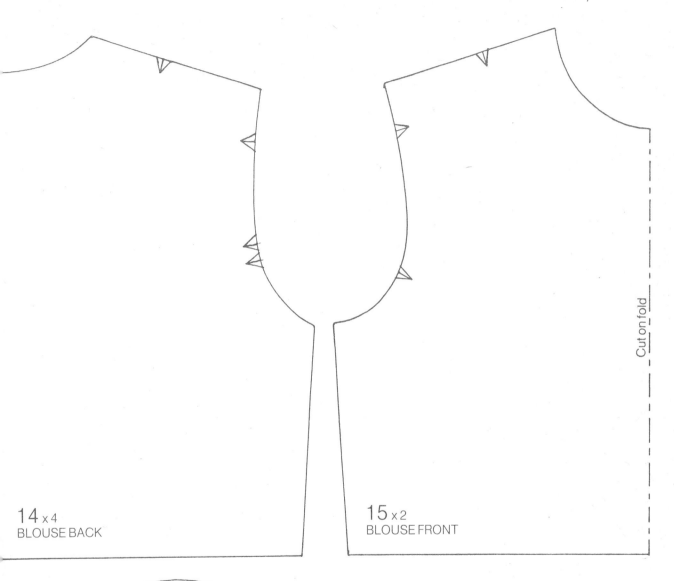

14 x 4
BLOUSE BACK

15 x 2
BLOUSE FRONT

Cut on fold

16 x 1
BACK FACING

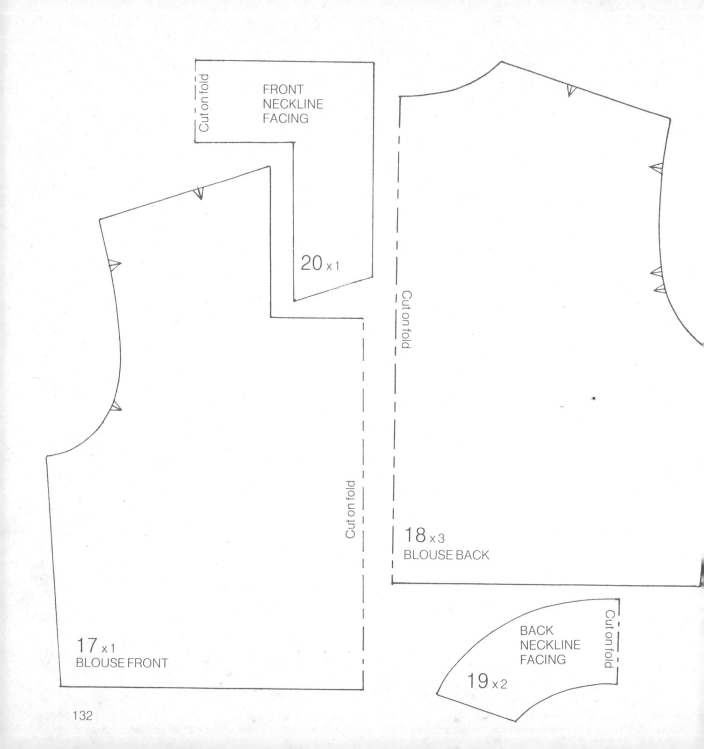

FRONT
NECKLINE
FACING

Cut on fold

20 x 1

Cut on fold

Cut on fold

18 x 3
BLOUSE BACK

17 x 1
BLOUSE FRONT

BACK
NECKLINE
FACING

Cut on fold

19 x 2

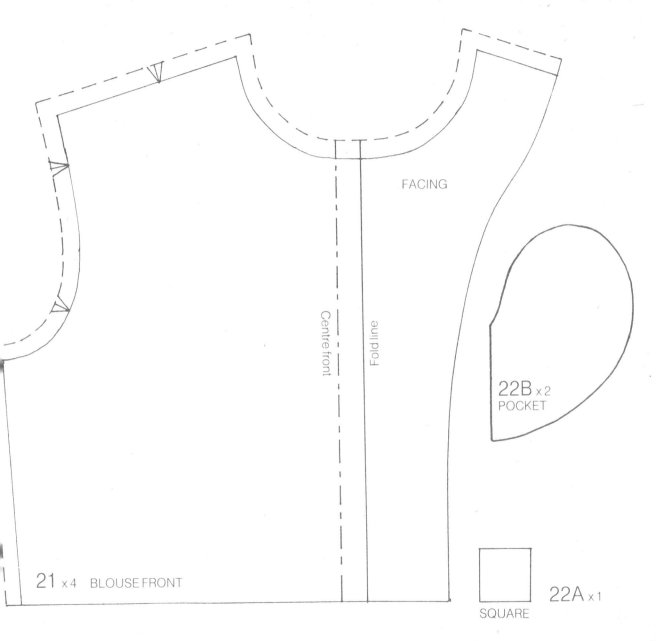

FACING

Centre front

Fold line

22B x 2
POCKET

21 x 4 BLOUSE FRONT

22A x 1

SQUARE

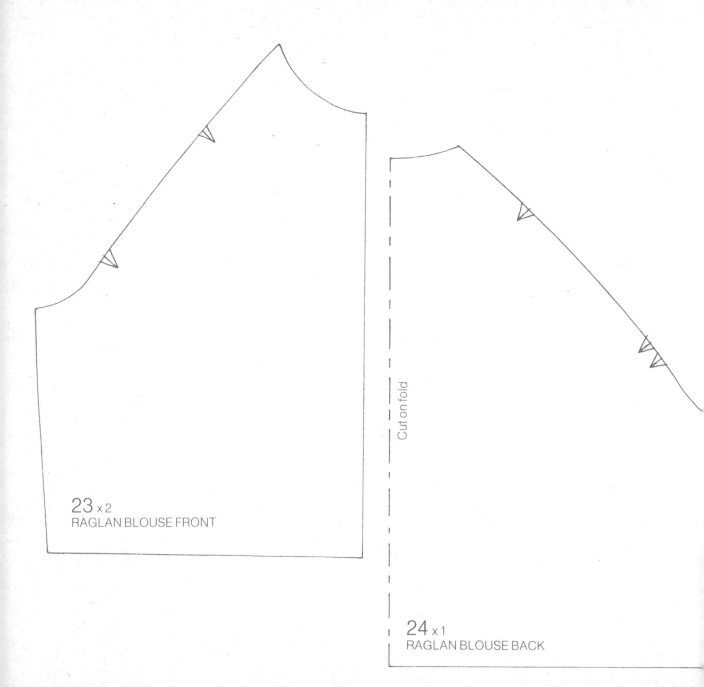

23 x 2
RAGLAN BLOUSE FRONT

Cut on fold

24 x 1
RAGLAN BLOUSE BACK

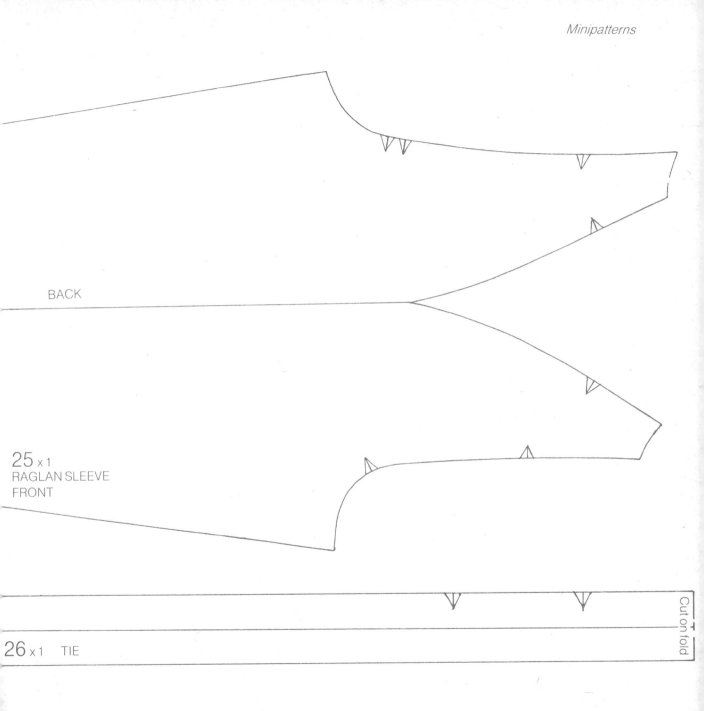

BACK

25 x 1
RAGLAN SLEEVE
FRONT

26 x 1   TIE

Cut on fold

Cut on fold

28 x1
CUFF

KIMONO SLEEVE

27 x2
FRONT AND BACK

Cut on fold

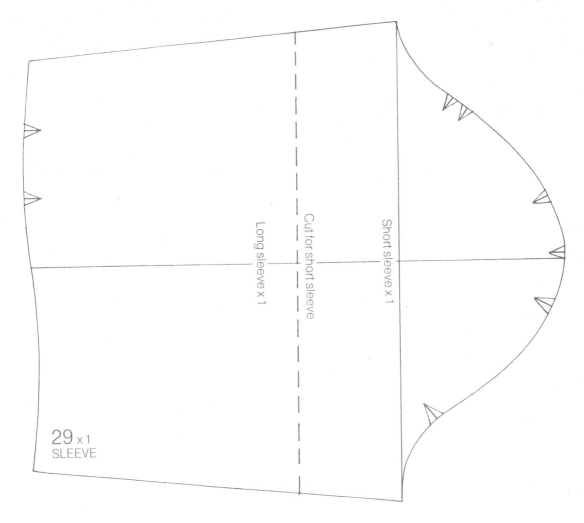

Long sleeve x 1

Cut for short sleeve

Short sleeve x 1

29 x 1
SLEEVE

30 x 1 STAND-UP COLLAR

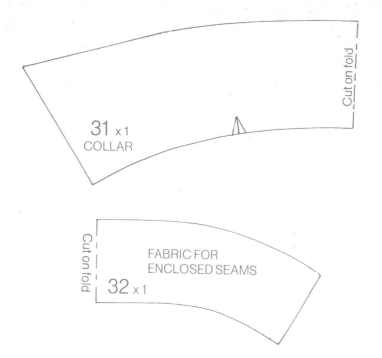

31 x 1
COLLAR

Cut on fold

Cut on fold

FABRIC FOR
ENCLOSED SEAMS

32 x 1

33 x 1
SQUARE POCKET

34 x 1
ROUND POCKET

The following instructions tell you how to use minipatterns to follow the dressmaking lessons, starting with Lesson 2 on the preparation of a pattern and fabric. The minipatterns are in numerical order, from page 127, and the number given for each cut-out refers to the number on the relevant minipattern.

You will need:

Tracing paper

A ballpoint pen

1 yard (1 metre) 36 inch (90 cm) wide mediumweight calico

Scraps of patterned fabric, or gift-wrapping paper

9 inches (25 cm) sew-on interfacing and 9 inches (25 cm) iron-on interfacing. You will need to use both types in Lesson 9; after that use whichever you prefer.

9 inches (25 cm) bias binding

18 inches (50 cm) grosgrain ribbon

18 inches (50 cm) lightweight fabric, suitable for lining

9 inches (25 cm) narrow tape, or strip of organza

Two zips, 4 inches (10 cm) long

Lesson 2: Preparation of pattern and fabric

Start to use the minipatterns. Use tracing paper to copy them, then treat them as you would ordinary commercial patterns, and follow the instructions in this lesson.

Lesson 3: Marking and cutting

Use the minipatterns, and calico

On each minipattern you will see the number of times it has to be cut out in calico. Make sure you cut it out the correct number of times, as you will need every piece.

Follow the instructions in this lesson, that is, mark, cut out and stay-stitch every one of your cut-outs.

You will need all of them, properly marked, in future lessons.

Use minipatterns for the section on working with patterned fabrics. Work with scraps of patterned material, or buy gift-wrapping paper—the more complex the design the better.

Lesson 4: Sewing stitches

No cut-outs are needed. Instead, cut strips of calico and use them to practise the stitches described in this lesson.

Lesson 5: Ironing and pressing

No cut-outs are needed. Practise with any pieces of fabric you have handy.

Lesson 6: Seams

Straight seams: cut-out 1
Curved seams: cut-out 3 (x 2)
Enclosed seams: cut-out 32

Lesson 7: Darts

Straight dart: cut-out 10
Curved dart: cut-out 10
Open dart: cut-out 10
Trimmed dart: cut-out 10

Lesson 8: Gathering

Material to be gathered: cut-out 2
Band: cut-out 4

Lesson 9: Interfacing

Fabric to be interfaced: cut-out 7 (x 2)
Cutting out sew-on interfacing: minipattern 7; interfacing (bought)
Cutting out iron-on interfacing: minipattern 7; interfacing (bought)
Interfacing half of the fabric piece: cut-out 5
Cutting out interfacing: minipattern 7; interfacing (bought)

Lesson 10: Finishing

Finishing light- or mediumweight fabric: cut-out 1
Finishing heavyweight fabric: cut-out 1; bias binding (bought)
To make your own bias binding: cut-out 8
French seam: cut-out 1 (x 2)
Curved seams: finish the curved seam you joined up in Lesson 6.

Lesson 11: Skirts

Skirt with waistband

Waistband: cut-out 13; ribbon (bought)
Straight skirt front: cut-out 6
Straight skirt back: cut-out 9 (x 2)

Make up your skirt. Join the centre back seam, leaving an opening for the zip.

Join the side seams and then follow the instructions in the lesson.

Skirt without waistband

Skirt: cut-out 11 (x 2); ribbon (bought)

Make up your skirt, leaving an opening for the zip at the centre back seam. Then follow the instructions in the lesson.

Lesson 12: Hemlines

Straight skirt: use the skirt you made up in Lesson 11 from cut-outs 6 and 9.
Full skirt: use the skirt you made up in Lesson 11 from cut-out 11.

Lesson 13: Necklines with facing

Round neckline

Blouse front: cut-out 15
Blouse back: cut-out 14 (x 2)
Front neckline facing: cut-out 12
Back neckline facing: cut-out 16

First make up your blouse. Join the two back pieces along the centre back seam. Leave open the space for the zip.

Join the front to the back at the shoulder seams and side seams, then follow the instructions in the lesson.

Square neckline

Blouse front: cut-out 17
Blouse back: cut-out 18
Front neckline facing: cut-out 20
Back neckline facing: cut-out 19
Square patch: minipattern 22A;
lightweight fabric (bought)

Make up the blouse but do not
leave an opening for a zip.
Then follow the instructions in the
lesson.

Lesson 14: Necklines with facing and front openings

Blouse front: cut-out 21(x 2)
Blouse back: cut-out 18
Back neckline facing: cut-out 19
Front neckline interfacing:
minipattern 21; interfacing
(bought)
Back neckline interfacing:
minipattern 19; interfacing
(bought)
Make up the blouse, then follow
the instructions in the lesson.

Lesson 15: Necklines with stand-up collars

Blouse front: cut-out 15
Blouse back: cut-out 14
Collar: cut-out 30
Collar interfacing: minipattern 30;
interfacing (bought)

Join the blouse front to the blouse
back at the shoulder seams, then
follow the instructions in the
lesson.

Lesson 16: Necklines with tie-collars

Blouse front: cut-out 21
Blouse back: cut-out 18
Tie-collar: cut-out 26
Tie-collar interfacing: minipattern
26; interfacing (bought)

Join the blouse front to the blouse
back at shoulder seams and side
seams, then follow the instructions
in the lesson.

Lesson 17: Necklines with facing and collar combined

Blouse front: cut-out 21
Blouse back: cut-out 14
Collar: cut-out 31
Collar interfacing: minipattern 31;
interfacing (bought)

Join the blouse front to the blouse
back at the shoulder seams, then
follow the instructions in the
lesson.

Lesson 18: Set-in sleeves

Short sleeve: cut-out 29

Set the sleeve in the armhole of
any of the blouses you have made.

Lesson 19: Raglan, kimono and dolman sleeves

Raglan sleeve
Blouse front: cut-out 23 (x 2)
Blouse back: cut-out 24
Sleeve: cut-out 25

Join at under-arm seams

Kimono sleeve

Blouse front and back: cut-out 27
(x 2)
Narrow tape or organza (bought)
for reinforcing curved seam

Dolman sleeve

This is like a kimono sleeve, but
the seam is not reinforced.

Lesson 20: Sleeves with cuffs

Long sleeve: cut-out 29
Cuff: cut-out 28
Cuff interfacing: minipattern 28;
interfacing (bought)

Follow the instructions in the
lesson. Set the sleeve in the
armhole of any of the blouses you
have made.

Lesson 21: Zips

Two zips, each 4 inches (10 cm)
long

Unpick the centre back seam in
the skirt with a waistband (Lesson
11) to 4 inches (10 cm). Insert one
of the zips. Unpick the centre back
seam in the blouse with a round
neckline (Lesson 13) and insert
the second zip.

Lesson 22: Pockets

The cut-outs for this lesson
are all large in proportion

to the skirts. This is to enable you to follow the instructions more easily.

Round patch pocket

Pocket: cut-out 33
Lining (bought)
Strip of calico

Follow the instructions in the lesson and attach the pocket to the calico.

Square patch pocket

Pocket: cut-out 34
Strip of calico

Follow the instructions in the lesson and attach the pocket to the calico.

Pocket in side seams

Pocket: cut-out 22B (x 2)

Unpick the side seam of the skirt with a waistband (Lesson 11) from the top of the pocket symbol until it is deep enough to take in the pocket cut-out. Follow the instructions in the lesson.

Lesson 23: Lining

Lining (bought)

Line one of the skirts you have made up.

Line one of the blouses you have made up.

Lesson 24: Buttonholes

2 pieces of calico, each 2 inches x 1 inch (5cm x 2.5 cm)
Organza (bought)
Strips of calico (for buttonhole lips)

Mark a buttonhole about 1 inch (2.5 cm) wide on the calico and follow the instructions in the lesson.

Index